APPRECIATION FOR ROD CHELBERG

"Not only has Dr. Chelberg spent decades of his life healing in the physical realm as a physician, but in this book he explores healing on a different level. Rod is a real-world, no-nonsense kind of guy who combines rigorous scientific training with an innate gift of connection with a Divine energy — enabling him to inspire and challenge readers of many backgrounds and beliefs. His medical career is expansive, including ICU, emergency medicine, hospice, and nursing home directorship, giving him a wealth of different perspectives within his own career in medicine. So when he speaks about what seem to be otherworldy concepts and occurrences, one feels a sense of authenticity and credibility and innocent wonder. Rod's accounts of witnessing people in the midst of loss and grief, on the edge of life and death, while experiencing extraordinary energies, visions, and miracles, brings forth a sense of being embraced by something infinite and being connected to each other and something much greater than what we thought we are on our own. What he shares in his book reflects this and could change your life." — KATJA VON TIESENHAUSEN, MD

"Dr. Rod Chelberg's exquisitely written memoir serves as a wonderful reminder that our spiritual path can bloom with grace and echo with laughter, as we remember the truth of who we are. His willingness and commitment to separate fearful fantasies from love's reality was instrumental in his own life, and universal to us all. His profound and personal connection to the Divine is presented in such a tangible way that we can't help but feel its immediate, healing presence with no need for delay."
— DANA MARROCCO PHD, author of *The Top Ten Lies We Tell Ourselves*

WHEN GOD CALLS, SAY YES!

A Physician's Experience of Mystical Guidance

by Rod Chelberg, MD

© Copyright 2019 by Rodney Chelberg Jr.

All rights reserved. No part of this book may be reproduced in any form or by any electronic or mechanical means without permission in writing from the copyright holder, except for the purposes of review. Scanning, uploading, and electronic distribution of this book is prohibited.

This book was produced in collaboration with Fearlesss Literary Services, which represents all subsidiary rights. Translation and republication inquiries can be directed to *info@fearlessbooks.com*.

ISBN: 978-1-7991537-7-1

Library of Congress Catalog Number
2019936735

Design & Typography
D. Patrick Miller
Fearless Literary Services
www.fearlessbooks.com

Cover Photograph
"Christ's Rose"
by William Almodovar

TABLE OF CONTENTS

PREFACE v

FOREWORD vii

INTRODUCTION 1

CHAPTER 1: Remembering Love 5

CHAPTER 2: Crash and Burn 19

CHAPTER 3: Floating 27

CHAPTER 4: Illumination 35

CHAPTER 5: Galaxy Walks 51

CHAPTER 6: The Unreality of Death 59

CHAPTER 7: Meeting God 87

CHAPTER 8: Extending Love 109

EPILOGUE 125

ACKNOWLEDGEMENTS 130

PREFACE

This memoir tells us of Dr. Rod Chelberg's lifelong journey of awakening to the Christ consciousness within himself, and within each of us. He travels from aloneness to feeling the need to belong to something larger than himself, gradually realizing that he will not find happiness by pursuing what the world names as sources of fulfillment, such as a successful career, marriage, home, and family.

For most of the book the author finds it more comfortable to relate to Christ, whom he feels standing close beside him, than to think about God. He gradually becomes aware of the limitations to intimacy with God that he learned as a youth in the Catholic Church.

A series of "crash-and-burn" events then open Dr. Chelberg to a whole new level of experience. He loses his home and family within a period of two years, his Dark Night of the Soul. Then comes what he calls "The Steps Up from the Bottom": discovering *A Course in Miracles* (ACIM), starting to do the daily lessons of the Course, learning to meditate in the rare quiet intervals that he finds while working in the Emergency Room, and finally discovering and connecting with key teachers of the Course, especially Dr. Kenneth Wapnick and Dr. Jon Mundy.

Subsequent chapters describe the many steps toward closeness (but not complete unity) with Christ, and a growing awareness of the complete non-humanness of God. By the last few chapters, Dr. Chelberg has grown totally comfortable with continually calling on Christ and God within himself for guidance.

Among the many stages of mystical awakening which the book touches upon are right-minded thinking, mind expansion, frame shifts, mind-quieting, space and time travel, the unreality of death, auras, unblocking the awareness of love's presence, illumination, the process of At-one-ment, and finally the love of God. Throughout these warm and personal revelations of Dr. Chelberg's experiences, we get to share in his growing awareness of his complete union with God.

The book ends with the final stage of mysticism, "The Extension of Love," in which God asks for help in healing the Sonship.

Dr. Chelberg returns over and over to the mind-altering process of meditation that enables him to experience many wonderful events and internal changes. He describes these mind changes and expansions in a language that is vivid and poetic, helping readers recognize that we, too, have had moments of our own closeness to Christ and to God.

— STEPHEN D. HOWARD, M.D.

FOREWORD

You're about to read a most extraordinary book. Although it is about God, it is not a theological book with intellectual speculations about God. It is one man's remarkable experience of God. Dr. Rod Chelberg is a man of medicine and a healer of mind, body, and soul. Rod and I became friends after our mutual friend Mari Perron, first receiver of *A Course of Love*, suggested to Rod that he pick up one of my books. Then, after a few email exchanges and calls between us, Rod came to a lecture I was giving in Portland, Maine.

That was the beginning of a series of further meetings, retreats, conferences and workshops we did together. Rod has also been my guest speaker many times at my monthly class in Manhattan based on *A Course in Miracles*. In October of 2018, I put together a three-day retreat, in part, just so folks could meet Rod.

We are all people of God; we can't help it. God created us; and having created us, God is also always in communion with us, whether we are aware of it or not. Lesson 49 from A Course in Miracles says, "God's Voice Speaks to Me All Through the Day." It's true, but then the Course also tells us that, while "All are called," "Few choose to listen." Our basic problem says, A Course in Miracles is "the authority problem." It's as though we say to God, "Thank you very much God but I would rather do it myself." As the Course expresses it, "Free will does not mean that you can establish the curriculum. It means only that you can elect what you want to take at a given time." [ACIM T-in.1:4-5] We don't listen because we "choose" not to — preferring to run the show ourselves.

After a "crash and burn" experience and then a giving-in to God, Rod began to pay more attention to the Voice for God in his meditations and in a quiet sinking into an awareness of the ever-consistent presence of God. In fact, Rod has been able to move into the presence of God with such constancy that a deep peace now literally emanates from him. Rod has chosen to listen and not simply to listen but to be able to act on what he hears.

Rod served as an emergency room doctor for fourteen years, followed by six years as a supervisor for several nursing homes and a hospice center. Among other things, this meant helping literally hundreds of folks in their transitioning from this world to the next. How lucky they were to have Rod as their caretaker and guide.

Rod used to go to church on a fairly regular basis. But later he found that, rather than taking the two hours to go to church, be there and then return home; he could move more deeply into his experience of God by meditating for a couple of hours on Sunday morning. Rod began to write about what occurred during these meditations, I was often able to open my email on a Monday morning to find a description of an incredible connection that occurred for Rod.

Rod had a mild stroke in November of 2016, which did not seriously impair his thinking or his ability to talk and had only a minor effect on his ability to walk. While the stroke did not impair his ability to communicate, it did mean, however, that he could no longer be a doctor. He could be a teacher for doctors but could no longer write prescriptions.

Sometimes a tragedy can be a blessing. Now, unburdened with the busy life of a hospital, Rod had time to sit down and do something that destiny had called upon him to do — write the book you are about to read.

One of the many takeaways from this book is the thought that what Rod has done we too can do. God is here [rather than "there"] waiting with infinite patience for his children to awaken, pay attention, remember home, and even more importantly, "come home" to a place we never left. We need only open to perceiving the presence of God in order to return home to God. Enjoy!

— Jon Mundy, Ph.D.

This book is dedicated to the Christ child that is within all of us, waiting for us to wake up and remember that we have always been eternally One with God.

*In the quietness of my mind,
As I rest in God, I remember,
I am peace, light and joy.
I am.*

INTRODUCTION

*W*HEN GOD calls, listen to the gentle voice of love that sings your name so softly. Love is calling to you. You are a being of love; pure, clean and innocent. A bright light for all to see.

When God calls, let go and accept your divine inheritance of love. There is nothing to do but this, surrender and enjoy the peace of His divine presence within you. Resonate in harmony with Him. Let His joined love flow to all who enter your presence.

When God calls, open up and trust that "All is well." You stand in the perfection of Divine Love that casts the shadow of your life aside, so that all you see is the brilliance of white light. All is God, all is light.

When God calls, say "Yes" to the beloved! Your life will change as the rosebud sheds its husk and blossoms into a beautiful flower. Your beauty and fragrance will bless all who come to see you and will bring them joy.

When God calls, be at peace, for you are at home, safe and forever one with Divine Love.

Mysticism, or Waking Up

Mysticism was my process of waking up from this dream world, that is, becoming liberated from the limiting thoughts of my ego consciousness. Once freed, I remembered that God and I are One; I am a divine, individualized extension of God manifesting as a person here in this world. I am Christ consciousness. Once my concepts of fear and guilt were gone, I was free to accept conscious union with God. As I practiced meditating and learning not to react to the distractions of the human world, I was able to hear His voice. I learned that when I said "Yes to God," and truly desired to wake up, it actually happened.

"The goal of mysticism is the attainment of realization of one's self as **Self** (Christ consciousness), so that life is a continuing experience of the Self. The attainment of the mystical estate is, of course, the ascension out of the personal sense of life into the experience of life lived as a universal and the divine." Joel Goldsmith, *A Parenthesis in Eternity*

I want to share with you my story of waking up (awakening) and remembering who I truly am — and what it is like to walk with the divine, or as revealed to Moses, the "I Am that I Am." Since I undertook this journey, I've been subtly guided back to the realization that the divine resides within my Heart. The bond to the "I Am" can never be broken, and thus we are always connected to our True Source in God.

During this waking up process, I had a number of mystical experiences and was able to help many people with their transition from this temporary dream of separation to our True Reality of light, love and spirit. Being here in this material world is only a temporary illusion. We are still one with God in Heaven and we are only dreaming that we have left home for a while.

I also hope that by sharing my story and experiences with you, you too will find the inspiration to wake up and remember that you were created from an extension of God's love, and that you are still one with Him in Heaven as well.

We are God. God is us. God is you and God is me. God is...

CHAPTER 1

Remembering Love

SINCE childhood I have felt a longing to connect to something that felt like home. I felt displaced and disconnected here in this world, empty and unsatisfied. This was a very deep feeling of hunger within me, coming from within my heart. In reality I was yearning to reconnect with God, but I was poorly taught by society, parents, and friends to focus on building a career, buying a home, and starting a family. In other words, I was taught to look outside myself for happiness. Along the way I developed a sense of identity or self which is called the "ego."

Within this false sense of myself, I learned that I was separate from others, that I was a body, and I had a personal life. This was my conventional identity as a human being. The ego became my only guide, teaching me that I separate from others and from God. Finally, I was led to believe that by pursuing only goals outside myself, I would likewise find happiness outside myself. By achieving my goals, I would finally be fulfilled, happy, and at rest. I would be at home.

However, despite obtaining a very nice house, and having a loving wife and family plus a solid medical career, there was still an unsatisfied feeling deep within me that this world could not fulfill. I could not escape the feeling that this world was somehow not my real home.

When I finally realized that this sense of longing was actually God seeking me, I stopped looking in the outside world and asked Him to help me find my way back to my true Home. This happened in 1996, while sitting in church just before an Easter service. From the pews I looked at all the finery, the altar, and the cross. It was then that I asked the Divine for His help because I wanted to know His thoughts.

Over time, I found that the Divine was already there within my heart. To paraphrase *A Course in Miracles*, "I need do nothing except extend a little willingness to relearn and remember who I truly am." I learned to look within to find true happiness and peace. That required unlearning the world of the ego, looking only for external gratification.

I call this process Illumination, and it is not the same thing as enlightenment to me. I had to recognize that Love is already within me, and that I did not need any intermediaries like churches, gurus or priests. I simply needed to remove my blocks to love's presence, and with Christ's Help I did just that. I now let God's love extend from my heart into this world. In so doing, I'm still in a dream world, but at least it is a happy dream and I am at peace.

My Journey

In 1969, Sir Alastair Hardy wrote a book entitled *The Flame*. In his research, he asked several thousand people what caused their entry into mystical experience. Out of 21 different causes, 183 of 1000 people responded that despair and depression was their primary cause —the most common answer given by far.

It seems that I needed something drastic to occur in my life before I could wake up and remember that God and I are one. Like many mystics before me, I chose the "crash-and-burn experience," analogous to the process of a forest fire. As it turns out, there are certain seeds that can only germinate under the intense heat of a fire. Without it, they will never grow. Once the fires are extinguished, new plants gradually repopulate and renew the forest. I call this intense burning process "God's Holy Fire."

Within my heart, God planted a seed of Himself, but I covered it with a thick layer of beliefs born of the ego. It was the intense fire of a crash-and-burn experience that destroyed the ego's shell around my heart. I lost my family and my home in a matter of a few months; my world came crashing down all around me and I was left with the depression, despair, and isolation for a period of two years. In the spiritual literature, this is called "the Dark Night of the Soul." I truly bottomed out, and it was then that Christ helped me ascend back into the light of God's love. (This story is told in detail in the next chapter.)

It was also during this time that I found *A Course in Miracles,* and began to study it every day. I would write the daily lessons on notecards and keep them in my pocket, reading them as often as I could during an ER shift or at home. I also started meditating as a means to quiet my mind. In that quiet I could feel the presence of Christ on my right side, growing stronger over the next several years. He became my guide and guided me in both the material and spiritual realms.

My mystical journey of waking up comprised three phases. The first I named "Illumination," as mentioned above. During this time that I recognized the unreality of this world and the reality of our true home that we call Heaven. I also learned to remove the ego limits on what I believed in. The second phase I call the "Atonement," during which I became one with God. During the third phase, "The Extension of Love," God asked me to help heal the world.

I have now learned to become unattached to this world, or at least not distracted by it. I practice peace with every step and maintain a constant awareness of God's presence. Since I'm still here, with Christ as my constant companion, I now walk in what the Course calls the "Happy Dream."

Terminology

The ego is a false sense of who I am: a body with a human mind and personality, separated from God. The ego is illusory, and truly insane. As I unlearned the ego, I started to develop mystical or spiritual senses that I will talk about later.

"I Am" is the name of God as He revealed himself to Moses. I Am consciousness is the same as Christ consciousness, and is my True Self as a spiritual being of light. It is a pure thought of love in the mind of God, where I am one with God.

I symbolize this union as follows:

S

GOD

N

God is cause, and we are His effect. We are equal to God in all respects except one: we did not create God; God created us. Otherwise we have all of God's creative powers to create, heal, and love. Just as the letter "O" is in the center of both words, we are all joined together in His divine center as "Oneness." It is through this center that God's love flows through me into this world. It is the opening to the channel of my heart.

Self refers to the Divine Spirit or "I Am." The lower case "self" consists of a limited human concept of who I am, what you see as a body with a personality when you meet me here in this world as Dr. Rod Chelberg. This is a false sense of who I truly am and it is only my identity here in this world. Dr. Rod Chelberg is based on an illusion.

The body is the ego's chosen home, existing in this dream world in either male or female form. As the Course explains, "The body no more dies than it can feel. It does nothing. Of itself it is neither corruptible nor incorruptible. It is nothing. It is a result of a tiny, mad idea of corruption that can only be corrected." [ACIM T-19.IV.C.i.5:2-6]

The world is an illusion, another separation device against God. It is a stage on which this body can act out its life's drama. Being unreal and not created by God, the world will disappear once we withdraw our thoughts from it. I have seen the end of the world in one of my meditations — and responded with a shrug of the shoulders and a smile. I watched it spin into nothingness and wondered, "What was that?"

A Course in Miracles is an individualized self-study course in mind training, channeled by Dr. Helen Schucman and scribed by Dr. Bill Thetford. I will abbreviate it to "ACIM" from now on.

The Etheric Realm is an area between the material world and the spirit world. When I visit this realm, I see millions of souls that seem to be stuck here. The background is the color of evening twilight, and I see no other objects similar to what we see in this world.

Light is our true essence as spiritual beings. It is pure, clear energy vibrating at an incredible rate of speed. It flows as a sphere of energy and it is experienced as peace, love and joy. Worldly light is generated by the sun, comprising photons in a stream. The light of God is different, having qualities of oneness, understanding and peace.

Atonement is conventionally defined as making amends, that is, paying or praying in order to apologize to God for our sins, with the hope that we are forgiven. Another common definition is the redemption of humanity achieved by the death of Jesus. These are traditional definitions, but not the idea I am referring to in this book. I redefine it as "At-One-Ment," meaning that we are at one with God. To atone, I need do nothing except wake up and remember that I Am in Truth — always One with God, always one with my Source.

Faith means believing and trusting in something unseen. I pray and meditate daily and I know that my true prayer is heard by Christ; he returns my faith to me as help and healing. Because of His help, I have gained confidence, trust and conviction in my faith. It has matured into the knowledge that God and I are One, that I am connected to my Source, and that I live by God's grace. I now walk in the "Light of God," and see everything fresh and new.

"Take the first step in faith. You don't have to see the whole staircase, just take the first step." — MARTIN LUTHER KING, JR.

Doubt means turning away from God and walking into the darkness of fear, another of the ego's chosen homes. As I will talk about later, we are constantly tricked into believing that the doubt we feel is real. Doubt creates mountains that we believe we must overcome. We forget that these barriers are only illusions in our mind, created with the ego's false guidance.

Christian terminology

I also use some terminology common to Christianity, but with different definitions. For example, I believe Jesus was a man who woke up, just as we all can, and remembered that he was in fact God's consciousness. For me, the image of Christ was initially easier for my mind to accept than God, because I was afraid of God. I was told by the Catholic Church that I was born with "original sin," and that somehow I had to appease God in order to win His favor and avoid landing in hell. I had to atone for my sins somehow. So, Christ was easier for me to accept as my brother.

My new terminology is as follows: God = Christ = Self = the Holy Spirit, and all this equals the "I Am." God-consciousness is manifested in this dream world as you, me, and everything around us. Despite the appearance of our different forms, we are all One in His Divine Mind. We are, in Truth, all One. In fact, there is only one of us here.

As you read on, you will see that I am very fluid about exchanging the words **God, Father, Christ** and the **Holy Spirit** with each other, for they're all the same to me. Our human minds need different definitions to maintain the separation of ideas. In religious tradition, each entity seems to have its own special functions. However, as you read my story of waking up, you'll find that Oneness transcends all these terms. Ultimately I cannot explain God with human language.

The varieties of "God"

During my childhood, the word "God" was derived from the Old Testament. But I now think of this as the ego's God, made in our human image yet externalized. The Old Testament taught me that this was a God of duality who believed in good and evil. He was above me in the clouds, up in Heaven, and we were fundamentally separate from each other. That God could be angry and vengeful and thus I should fear His mighty wrath.

The church taught me that I should pray to God to help solve my problems and lead me to safety. I always hoped that this external God would indeed help me, and that during these times I would be good enough for Him. Now I see this is a Santa Claus version of God, who requires certain rituals and other appeasing behaviors. Finally, I was raised to believe that I needed a hierarchy of clergy and a church in order to reach this God; I certainly could not do so by myself.

As I came to learn, this ego "God" has no power at all and is only an illusion.

Our ideas of God are all based on human concepts, projected onto a divine figure. Thus it seems that there are many different types of Gods depending on one's religious beliefs, including Hindu, Muslim, and Christian. Yet God has no human attributes at all. Even to say "God is love" is incorrect because we each have a different interpretation of love. Consequently we would have a God of multiplicity, but this is impossible, for God is Oneness. However, I do say that God is love, peace, and joy simply because these are among the best descriptions of God that I can use given the limitations of our human language. God is... and that is all I can really say.

The traditional God is associated with masculinity. For example, God is portrayed as a male by Michelangelo in the Sistine Chapel, where He is portrayed touching the finger of Adam. But in Reality, this is not true. There is no gender associated with the divine just as there's no gender associated with electricity, sunlight, or gravity. They just are what they are.

I was taught to fear God, for He was always judging me as good or bad. This "fear of God" is similar to how a dictator is regarded by his subjects. But God treats us all with equality; He is completely impersonal and exercises no discernment or judgment. God's light shines on us all equally at all times, and we are always connected to our Source. God does not see our dream lives here. He sees only Himself there within your mind, there within your heart.

When you become one with God on this mystical journey, you wake up! When that happens, all your limited concepts and beliefs are stripped away and you feel totally free. Realizing the falseness of your human concepts, you become aware that you are a thought of pure love in God's infinite Mind. You see only your own innocence and purity.

In so doing, you will also realize that you and God are one, with no separation or distinction of any kind. There are no boundaries anymore, only a sense of fullness, expansiveness and peace. There is only "I." All doubt will be removed from your mind and you will know the truth of what I say.

God is now very personal to me, and I converse with Him as casually as I do with a true friend. God is so very loving, gentle and kind, and that's how I know who I really am: this loving child, the Christ Child.

The God Experience

God can only be known through experience. We can read about God all we want, but it is not the same as experiencing God as I Am. When I became one with God, I experienced love, peace, and joy all at the same time. God is... and we cease to speak, because human language cannot describe God. We use words like awe, rapture and ecstasy in a very poor attempt to describe what it is like to become one with God.

Until you have tasted an orange, there is no way that I can explain to you what it is like. I can describe it as best I can, but until you know the taste, we might just argue about it. Once you have experienced the flavor, then we can share our experience of it.

Christ

I first started to notice Christ as an invisible presence on my right side during medical school, my internship and residency. Usually I felt this presence when somebody was dying, and the experience brought us all comfort. A feeling of peace and love radiated from Him to me, making me very calm and peaceful. My patients and their family members also became peaceful during this time of transition.

Over time, I started to hear Christ's voice very clearly telling me what to do, and then I started to see His presence here in this world. He appeared as a pinkish red aura in a bead shape, about four feet tall upright, resting about a foot off the ground. I have learned to ask for His advice and let Him go before me in difficult situations. Nowadays I feel His presence constantly, on my right side and in my heart.

Later, when I visited the Etheric Realm, Christ appeared to me as a light, cloudy white human form. This is the only time I see Him in this manner.

In Heaven, Christ is only a clear thought that I am aware of. I too am a clear thought of awareness, as is God. Everything there is in a clear, dimensionless space with a background of a brilliant formless white light.

The Holy Spirit

The Holy Spirit is synonymous with the voice of God that I hear in this world or in my meditations. His voice is always quiet, loving and gentle when He speaks to me, as you'll see in the poems and short quotes that were given to me over time.

As an analogy, when my son Brad was very young and having a bad dream, I could usually hear him in his restless sleep. I did not know what he was dreaming about but I knew he was upset. As I opened the door, a small amount of hall light would shine on his face. I would quietly walk up to him, place a hand on his shoulder and say, "Daddy is here, you are safe, and I love you." Though Brad would not wake up, he would settle down from his bad dream and fall back into a deep sleep.

Whether I hear the voice of Christ, the Holy Spirit, or God, it is all the same voice helping me to understand that my dreams of upset are only illusions. If I calm down and allow the Holy Spirit's voice to enter my dream, my perceptions of it change and I am healed. A miracle has occurred, leaving me with gratitude and peace.

The Son of God or the Sonship

During my lectures, people sometimes take offense at the idea of a Sonship, that is, that we are all "Sons of God" together. As I stated before, there is no gender to God and there is no gender associated with the word "Son" in this reference. The Sonship includes all of us whether we are male or female. God knows not of our dream of duality, of being male or female. He only knows us as He knows Himself, as love. However, I do the best I can with this limited human language. So I try to clarify that we are all the Children of God, and each of us is an individual manifestation as a Child of God.

As a comparison, I think of the Sun as a symbol for God. In this world, I am a sunbeam extending out from God into the universe, or perhaps one photon particle. However, in Reality I am not an individual particle, always being connected to God by a thin silver cord. I can never be separated from God even though I may think this has happened. As the Course puts it, I am still home in Heaven with God and merely dreaming that I am in a world of separated duality.

Grace

Grace is synonymous with the flow of God's Love through me. I see Grace as a creamy white light, and experience its movement through my heart as a pleasant and delicious sensation. I feel joy when this happens.

Our True Home

Our true home is within. We are One with the Divine in His Infinite Mind, or Heaven. God is always calling us home with our every breath and heartbeat. We need only to quiet our minds in order to hear His gentle voice of love and know that this is so.

In addition to telling my story, I will share a few personal letters to friends about these mystical experiences, as well as some short poems and stories. Anything italicized is my own Christ-inspired writing that is my gift to you, to help remind you of who we all truly are.

I apologize if I repeat myself, but it's sometimes necessary because the ego puts up so many defenses against our remembrance that we are each an individualized representation of Christ consciousness, appearing symbolically on this earthly plane. God is constantly calling you home to remember who you are. Eventually, when you hear God calling to you, you can simply say "Yes" and He will do the rest...

I Am the Christ Child

I am the Christ Child, born fully pure and innocent from the thought of God's Love.

I am the Christ Child, the Son of a wholly loving Father. Splendor and glory are always within me as gifts from God.

I am the Christ Child, fully awake, and One with God and all that I see. I see only reflected love in you and me, because together we are as One.

I am the Christ Child, and I am healed as I remember these thoughts, free at last from guilt and fear.

I am peace. I am Love. I am perfect.

I am the Christ Child.

CHAPTER 2

Crash and Burn

In the spring of 2004, I was appointed to be the new medical director of St. Joe's emergency room in Bangor, Maine. I was very pleased with this promotion, feeling that I had finally arrived and was entering into a highlight of my professional career. In addition, my family lived in a very comfortable home in a small town one hour south of Bangor. My two boys were doing well in school and we were solidly connected with our community. My wife seemed content at the time. We had been married 17 years with occasional minor bumps along the way, but nothing that I considered serious.

My wife and I had 'adopted' an elderly woman around the year 2000. First she was a good friend, eventually becoming part of our family as our pseudo-grandmother. She was loving, kind and funny. We invited her to all of our family holidays and often went to church together. All in all, it was a nice time in my life.

One day in the summer of 2004, my elderly friend pulled me aside and intimated her concern that my wife was involved with another man. He too was another good friend of our family. Denial was my first reaction. But when I asked my wife, she stated that it was all true and that she no longer loved me. Despite three months of counseling, she remained adamant about a divorce.

In the fall, my wife asked me to leave our home. I moved out and stayed with some friends in Bangor for a while. In their small guest room, I felt as if I was in a prison cell — isolated, hopeless, and fearful of the future.

We moved forward from separation to divorce in a very short period of time after I left our home. I felt profoundly hurt and betrayed by my wife and former friend. I was confused by this stormy whirlwind of change, feeling guilty and responsible although I didn't understand what had happened. I thought I must have not loved her deeply enough, or she would have stayed. The grief and loss persisted after the divorce settlement, the starting point of a long depression.

In the meantime, my former friend moved into our family home with my family. Shock, bewilderment and anger were added to my chaotic feelings, and I was having difficulty concentrating on work. For that matter, grocery shopping seemed overwhelming. Eventually I bought a home in Bangor so my boys could visit with me every other weekend.

A second traumatic development came in the summer of 2005. My oldest son called to tell me they were moving to Virginia Beach, 1500 miles away. They were leaving that very day, and there was nothing I could do about it. This was a complete shock, because I had essentially lost my boys. I filed for custody and began the arduous task of court hearings. I started having panic attacks and my depression was getting worse; my professional focus was worse than ever as my mind was starting to freeze up.

When we had our first custody hearing, my ex-wife easily won. In Maine, only ten per cent of fathers get custody of

2: Crash and Burn

their children. Now I had even more limited access to my boys because they were so far away. Later that year, when I went to visit them in Virginia Beach and saw the school they would attend, I was horrified. The school was crowded and congested, rife with gangs and drug abuse. My two little boys would not survive in a culture like this, and I was powerless to protect them. But I would not tolerate my boys living in this environment so I filed for a second custody hearing hiring a guardian ad litem (a person who investigates the best interests of children in a custody case) to help.

Fear and depression were my daily companions now, as my mind was constantly spinning despite medications and counseling. I was becoming exhausted. An internal, seemingly eternal anguish had settled deep within me, worse than any physical pain I have ever felt before. Nothing helped ease the distress.

One Saturday morning I woke up crying, desperate to end the pain. As I walked into the kitchen, I stared at the array of knives in the block on the counter. I suddenly had my answer. I took off my shirt and looked at my chest; I could see where the apex of my heart was tapping against my chest wall, causing a slight movement in the skin. I pulled a long sharp knife out of the knife block and placed the tip of it against my left chest wall. I angled the knife into the correct, deadly position and placed both hands over the handle of the knife. I knew that with one quick upward thrust, my life would be over instantly and I would be free of all pain.

As I stood there crying, anticipating the end of my life, Christ gently whispered in my right ear and said, "Let's go for a walk first." I felt His strong, loving presence right by my side.

I put the knife back on the counter top and put on some new clothes, then went outside and walked for about a half mile on that sunny Saturday morning. Despite the walk, my mind was still spinning and I could not get it to stop.

When I reentered my kitchen, I was still crying and I was still drowning in awful emotions. I felt empty and alone once more. I took my shirt off and again placed the knife tip against my chest wall where my heart apex was.

But Christ spoke very clearly for a second time into my right ear. "Let's go for another walk." Again I obeyed, and this time I could feel His arm around my shoulders, and the warmth of His loving presence entered me. I felt soothed and taken care of. My mind was starting to settle down and become clearer. As we walked, my pain was starting to decrease. Continuing on, He said, "Everything is going to be okay. Your boys are going to need you very soon." I was calmed by His words and His presence.

Realizing I could not get by alone anymore, I sobbed, "Please help me." I surrendered my will, let go of my problems and relaxed into His love, deciding to trust Christ above all. Once I did that, a seed of hope was planted in my heart. For the first time in over a year, my perception changed. As I looked around, I saw how beautiful everything was, and knew somehow that everyone was going to be taken care of. This was the first major turning point of my spiritual life. I did not have to carry this heavy burden by myself anymore; Christ was going to help me. I was enormously relieved.

With each day, I felt more hope, less pain and less depression. I felt compelled to read spiritual literature and to also start meditating every day in order to calm my mind. These two practices greatly helped me stay centered and peaceful. I was guided to find A Course in Miracles and began reading it every day. Soon it seemed that this course would not let go of me, and it became my guidebook for every step through life.

A few months later, I was watching a movie called "Nanny McPhee" where an angel disguised as an English nanny helps some children and their single father marry a scullery maid, against all odds. At the end of the movie when the couple was getting married, Christ said to me, "There are angels watching over you." My faith then turned to knowledge and I suddenly knew that I was going to win my custody case against all odds. This eventually happened, though not without some bumps in the road.

My boys were visiting in the fall of 2004 in my new Bangor home. One day I decided that I wanted to start a fire in the fireplace while we played Monopoly in the living room. I cleaned the ash out from the fireplace and poured it into my 30-gallon trash bucket inside the garage. Unbeknownst to me, there were hot embers in the ash that caused a fire, burning a third of my garage down by the time the fire department put it out. My home was on the news, and I knew that this disaster could be used as ammunition against me in custody proceedings.

But the fire was ruled as an accident and I received a large sum of money from the insurance company to pay for repairs. As I like to build houses, throughout the next year, I cleaned the damage away and a friend helped me rebuild the garage. When I looked at the burned-out shell of the garage, I had a moment of divine inspiration: "Build a second story over the garage and create a new living space for your boys." I could actually see the new addition above the garage, and soon it became a reality.

When we had our second custody hearing in 2007, the new judge ruled in my favor that my boys would have a better life staying in Maine with me. Relief and happiness filled my heart, and I cried with joy as we drove home to our new home in Bangor. They moved in to live with me through college. I was content knowing that they would be with me. I showed them the new recreation room above the garage, telling them that this space was entirely theirs and that they never had to fear this type of loss and upset again in their lives. I would be there for them.

In a short time, both were involved with music and sport, and started to make new friends in a good school. Their old friends would come up to visit for a day or a weekend, or I would take them down to our former home and they could visit with their friends down there. They settled into their new life with me quite nicely. Every weekend, the house was filled with my boys and their friends. This lasted from middle school all the way through college. In our first few years together, on Sunday evenings after a day of playing, we would have pizza and then watch a movie together. My boys would sit on either side of me with my arms around them and many times they gently dozed off. I felt content and thankful to have them in my life. A very strong bond of love developed between the three of us during this time, and I felt whole again.

Problems

When I have a problem, I need faith.
When I have faith, I trust.
When I have trust, Love flows.
When I have Love flowing, I am calm.
When I have calm, I am quiet.
When I have quiet, I can hear God.
When I have God, I remember we are one.
When I have oneness, I am at peace.
When I have peace, I have no problems.

CHAPTER 3

Floating

When I was fourteen, I first heard these lyrics from the Moody Blues song "Floating:"

Floating free as a bird
Sixty foot leaps it's so absurd
From up here you should see the view
Such a lot of space for me and you
Oh you'd like it
Gliding around get your feet off the ground
Oh you'd like it
Do as you please with so much ease
Now I know how it feels
To have wings on my heels
To take a stroll among the stars
Get a close look at planet Mars

As I listened to this song, it occurred to me how wonderful it would be to float among the stars as suggested, so I decided to try it.

In my darkened bedroom, I lay down on my bed and closed my eyes. I slowed my breathing down and imagined myself floating out of my body with ease. A feeling of peacefulness and security descended upon me. I felt incredibly light inside and to my surprise, I did float out of my body. Then I could see a whitish outline of my body and I could also see the room that I was in. I rotated around and looked at myself lying on the bed as if asleep, but I knew I was not. This was my first experience with astral projection.

Thereafter I could always lie down, relax, and allow this peaceful sensation to flow over me. I always experienced such incredible feelings of lightness and freedom, with no sense of any human limitations. I could not hear or feel anything, but I still knew what was going on around me. It was during these excursions that I realized I was only a pure thought of consciousness, or self-awareness. I usually stayed in my room floating above my body for usually an hour or so. I felt so comfortable in this space that I did not want to go back into my body, enjoying what I called "clear light."

In time, I would travel farther and take little trips around the house or our yard. It became a game, as I could see what was going on around me but I knew that no one could see me.

Once I took a trip to Paris. I was floating perhaps ten feet over an outdoor café in springtime, and the trees were in bloom. People were sitting at round tables with red and white checkered tablecloths. I could see them eating their meals, and I saw others walking around and enjoying themselves. When I looked down the street, I saw the Eiffel tower in the distance several miles away. The whole scene was beautiful and I was thoroughly enjoying this trip.

Spiritual vision

During this time, I also started to develop my spiritual vision.

I still saw everything with my human eyes, but in my forehead region, commonly called the third eye, I started to experience a secondary vision. This new way of seeing was intermittent and I could not command it to appear. But when it was present, I saw the life force within all things. Everything was in various shades of white on white with small gold flecks moving within the form of whatever I was looking at. The air was faintly white whereas a tree was densely white. To this day, I still occasionally see everything as different densities of white on white. I now know that what I was seeing was the life force that is within us and everything around us.

Early meditations

In addition to these wonderful experiences, I started to meditate, without formal training, learning by trial and error. I would sit in a comfortable chair with a blanket, in a dark and quiet room. I learned to control my breathing by slowing it down, and evening out my inhalations and exhalations. At first I had a lot of random thoughts that interfered with my meditation, but then I learned how to breathe through them and not be distracted.

Over the next several years of practice, I trained my mind to become quiet and focused, keeping my attention centered on my forehead above my eyes. As I progressed, a deep calmness and peace would settle upon me. Time no longer mattered and for a while I felt whole and complete. I realized this was a very comfortable place to be.

In junior high, I became a long-distance runner. I quickly learned to meditate and run at the same time. I developed the habit of a runner's high and could easily do ten miles with no effort at all. Time and space seem to stop when I ran, feeling disconnected from my body. I just floated along with it in a state of serene peace and joy. Later, in high school, I started running twice a day. What I noticed was that the peace I obtained during the morning run would stay with me throughout the day and then be reinforced with the longer run later in the day. This meditative state kept me focused on the thought of peace all day long.

Silent Unity

It was during high school that my mother introduced me to Silent Unity and Daily Word, both produced by Unity Worldwide Ministries. I thoroughly enjoyed reading the Daily Word messages. I started to read many of the Silent Unity authors such as Charles and Myrtle Fillmore, Eric Butterworth and James Dillet Freeman. They taught that we were the creators of our life experiences, and thus we could change our life by changing our thoughts. I wanted to understand how to do this.

Swami Rama

In my last year of high school, in the 1970s, a friend introduced me to Swami Rama at his retreat center in Chicago. I thought he was a very kind, spiritual man and I could feel his life force reaching out to me. He pulled me aside one day into his private office where we had a very nice discussion about life, and he gave me a string of mala beads, a personal mantra, and instructions on using both.

About six months later, I went with my friend to a second yoga retreat with Swami Rama. There were perhaps 100 people gathered around him, and as we entered the room, he raised his hands above his head in a warm greeting. The crowd parted, and I saw his body surrounded by an aura of white light, with a red light centered on his heart. Initially I was stunned by this sight but then I felt the warmth of the love envelop me and I ran into his arms. I had never felt love like this before.

Over the ensuing week, during a lecture, he stopped to point me out and say, "You see that young man sitting over there, he is going to be a very fine doctor one day." My first thought was that this was a big mistake on his part. However, he pulled me into his office again later in the week to reinforce the idea that this was my destiny.

My first experience with Christ

Later that year, I had my first experience with Christ. I was flying my dad's 172 Cessna airplane on a clear blue summer day when I heard a machine gun hammering sound coming from my engine. When I looked at the instrument panel, it showed that I had lost all oil pressure, the engine temperature was critical, and the RPMs were starting to slow down. I knew that the engine was going to fail. Since the metallic pounding was getting worse, I decided to call an in-flight emergency.

At that moment, I felt a very warm, loving presence sitting in the copilot's seat. As I looked over, I saw a faint white aura of white light sitting there in the shape of a man. I knew deep down that it was Christ sitting next to me. He told me to put the microphone back in the cradle, and very clearly said, "Feather the prop." So I replaced the microphone and as I pulled back on the throttle, it seemed as if the airplane was being gently lifted up by a pair of hands under it. A deep sensation of peace and safety came over me, and I knew that everything was going to be okay despite the fact that I was fourteen miles short of the runway.

On our way back to the airport, Christ was looking around and appeared very content. He said, "It is a beautiful day to fly, isn't it?" I just looked at him and nodded my head yes. Fortunately, I made it back to the airport. But my engine did fail after I taxied off the runway and I had to be towed back to the hangar.

Quiet time

Over the next several years, I don't recall any mystical experiences, as I was very involved with college, working, and having relationships. These were great distractions for a while and I felt fulfilled as a person. I enjoyed setting goals and accomplishing them; I entered medical school and met a wonderful woman whom I later married. We started a family by having two boys.

The Color of Heart Auras

In the years that followed, during the early months of my Internal Medicine residency, I started to see auras around people's hearts. I could see three colors: green, red and blue. My heart area was always green, and I assumed this was the color of healing and of life. It is also the color of medicine. I interpreted blue to be the color of divine intelligence, and red to be the color of divine love.

On occasion, I would see clear auras or pure white auras surrounding a person's body. They seemed to be radiating this light from deep within, and somehow I knew they were very spiritual people. The only other color that I sometimes saw surrounding people was black. When I saw this aura, I knew that this person was going to die soon or experience significant difficulty in their lives.

One evening, in the early years of medical school, I was with a friend attending a play. As I was looking around, I saw this man with a black aura surrounding his body. I mentioned this to my friend and he immediately grabbed my forearm and said, "That's my uncle!" As it turned out, he had metastatic prostate cancer and he did not tell anybody about it. He died six months later.

This experience was very upsetting for me. So I decided that I did not want to see auras on people anymore and I did not want any more mystical experiences.

However, several years later I started having a different type of mystical experience. I was in my last year of residency when I was learning to take care of critically ill patients who were in the process of dying. I often felt that there was a presence entering the room with me, that brought peace to us all. I somehow knew that everything was going to be okay and that I had nothing to be afraid of. I started to feel a connectedness to everyone present, and a lightness in the room. My perceptions of time and space were altered; everything was momentarily suspended. I felt as if something was flowing through my heart. I didn't yet know what it was, but it was a beautiful sensation.

Once a patient expired, I would silently say the Lord's Prayer for my patient, asking that they would be taken home to heaven. I considered this to be my last act as a doctor to help my patient. When I could, I would touch the patient's hands or hold their hand to my heart as I prayed. The family felt peace and this peace stayed with the family members even after the funeral. I was often complimented by family members on how well I had taken care of their loved one; however I knew it was not me. I didn't know what it was exactly, but I was thankful to have the experience.

This sequence of events was going to become a very common practice for me in my later years. And in time, what was actually happening was explained to me.

God's Presence

In the silence of my mind, into the deepest recesses of solitude therein, I wandered. I looked at my memories of my time but I dared not stay there, for I was being called.

Deeper I ventured until I came upon holy ground. My mind was then filled with light, and my being was enlightened by grace. For here I found God waiting for me.

CHAPTER 4

Illumination

For me, illumination is primarily concerned with learning that peace is only found within myself and not in the outside world. As an analogy, I imagine myself as a 100-watt light bulb. As I grew up in this ego world, veils or curtains comprising who I should be and what I should achieve were placed over my light bulb like a lampshade. They dimmed my light to about 7 watts, so that I saw mostly darkness. Once I started on a mystical path, Christ helped me to remove these veils and my light became brighter. As a result, my spiritual senses became more apparent to me, and I started to see farther in both the human and spiritual dimension.

As I stated earlier, illumination is not the same as what some people think of as enlightenment. Early on, I believed that God and I were separate — hardly an enlightened state of being. But the unreality of this world of illusion was already becoming apparent to me. The light was dawning in my mind, and as I lightened up, all of the worldly concepts and beliefs that I had been taught began to fade. I could see much better, so to speak, as I started questioning what my ordinary senses were telling me. I was becoming free of the limitations of everyday reality.

Thus began the development of my three "Spiritual Senses."

First, I acknowledged an awareness of Christ's Presence next to me on my right side. When He was present, I would sometimes hear a faint click in the material world. For a split second time and space were altered, and after that, everyone around me was connected to Christ. I call this whole awareness process a "Frame Shift."

Next, I developed a second sensation of hearing; I could hear Christ's voice in my right ear, which I called a "Listening Ear."

Spiritual Vision was the third spiritual sense to fully develop, as I started to see auras around people in my mind's eye. Auras sometimes identified medical problems, as well as revealing the God energy that is the composition of all things. I also started to see the red aura of Christ in the emergency room.

Over time, all three senses began working together when I was treating patients. This process of integration of my spiritual senses enabled me to communicate more fully.

Frame Shifts

In grade school, we used to watch movies on projectors using metal reels. There were a multitude of pictures in sequence on celluloid film. When the film occasionally jumped the reel, the picture on the screen would shift, blur, or even burn up on the screen. (We always cheered when this happened.) In a similar manner, my vision shifts suddenly and I see the world from a new perspective. In what I call a "frame shift," time and space momentarily skip on the reel of life.

These subtle, sudden frame shifts are often preceded by a very soft "click." Over time, I became aware that these shifts are simultaneous with my becoming aware of Christ's presence.

In terms of the Course, these are "holy instants" where Christ reaches through the spiritual dimension to me, into this limited human dimension. It is a joining of my mind with the divine, the effect of which alters my perception of this human world.

Draw near to God, and he will draw near to you. — JAMES 4:8 , CSB

These frame shifts were my very first spiritual sense to develop, and are roughly equivalent to our human sensation of touch. Christ's presence is almost palpable when he enters into my awareness. It feels as if He is touching me on my right arm, and from that touch I become aware of Him near me.

I subsequently learned that before every mystical experience, I would have a frame shift. I suppose one could call this Christ knocking at the door. Once I open that door, a whole new line of communication is available to me. This is a spiritual form of communication, a joining of my mind and heart with Christ. Once joined, His presence extends from my heart to all those around me. This form of communication is silent and without words; we are all enveloped by a feeling of Oneness and deep peace. I know that we are all in the presence of something very holy and mystical.

A frame shift experience

One young woman was brought in to the emergency room with complaints of right lower quadrant abdominal pain. She found it difficult to walk, but had no nausea or vomiting. She was seen in another emergency room the previous day, where she was started on antibiotics. As she lay on the gurney, I saw a haunted look of pain and fear in her eyes.

As I talked to this young lady and her mother, a frame

shift occurred. I felt the presence of Christ entering the room, and as a result we all started to feel peace. As I looked down at her right side, I could see that she had acute appendicitis by the way she was positioned on the gurney. I touched her mother's right shoulder, but kept eye contact with my patient. I told them both of my diagnosis, and that very soon she would be pain-free with the medicines that I was going to give her. Upon talking to me, she immediately felt relief, as did her mom. I was happy for that. But in reality, it was the flow of Christ's love to them that brought them both relief from fear and pain, because she felt much better even before I gave her any medicine. Shortly thereafter, a CT scan of her abdomen was positive for acute appendicitis. She had surgery later that day and did very well.

Listening to Christ

The second spiritual sense I developed was the ability to hear Christ's voice in my right ear (only once on the left). Of course I always hear my own voice in my head, but I knew the source of this voice was not me. Christ speaks with great authority and I have never doubted what I heard. He always told me what was wrong with my patients and then gave me advice on how to treat them. It is very reassuring to me to get a "stat consult" with Christ standing next to me and whispering in my right ear, telling me what to do in order to help my patient. So many people's lives were saved as result of his help to me. Here are some examples.

Tylenol Poisoning: A middle-aged well-dressed woman was brought in by ambulance unresponsive and critical. The only history I obtained from the ambulance crew was that she collapsed at work. It is quite common to receive patients this way, without a clue as to what happened to them. As the ambulance crew and nursing staff started working on stabilizing her, Christ whispered that I should push on her right foot. As I did so, her foot reflexively tapped on my hand three times. Christ said, "See, she has Clonus" (an abnormal reflex that indicates poisoning to her brain). "She has Tylenol poisoning and this is causing her altered mental status. Order a stat Tylenol level and an ammonia level."

Now these are very special labs, not routine. My nurses thought I was crazy. However, within half an hour both labs came back critically high. I gave her the antidotes that ultimately saved her life.

I later found out that she was taking a painkiller with Tylenol in it, supplementing this medicine with over-the-counter Tylenol to help control her pain. Thus she was inadvertently taking lethal doses of Tylenol by mistake, leading to liver failure. That meant she could not clear her blood of the poisons that naturally accumulate in our blood. People usually die within three days from Tylenol poisoning, if they do not get the antidotes soon enough. But after a few days in the hospital, she was discharged to home.

A Young Boy: A 15-year-old boy was brought in by his parents in the early evening because he apparently passed out while running at school. They wanted to know if anything was seriously wrong. The child had mild abrasions but otherwise looked fine, and had no serious complaints except that he felt sore from falling. When I touched him, Christ told me, "This child has Metabolic Syndrome and he passed out because of an abnormal heart rhythm. Order a stat cardiac enzyme test.

He had an acute heart attack while running, producing the abnormal heart rhythm that caused him to fall."

Ordinarily I do not order cardiac enzymes to evaluate for a heart attack on 15-year-olds who happen to fall down. When the test results came back, they were extremely elevated and positive for an acute heart attack. This young man was admitted and started on cardiac medication; the following day, he was sent to Boston for follow-up care. He was ultimately found to have a 95% closure of his left main artery, a lesion known to doctors as the "widow-maker." Fortunately, they were able to put a stent in and save his life. By listening to Christ, I was able to start that rescue.

Misleading Chest Pain: A 45-year-old woman was out in the garden working when she developed mid-sternal chest pain. She described it as a tenderness where her ribs attached to the sternum on the left side. If she pressed on this area of her chest, she could reproduce her pain. She had no other cardiac symptoms or history. In the emergency room, the ambulance crew never did an ECG or heart tracing as they considered her a very low risk for a heart attack. Everyone was thinking that she merely strained her chest wall.

However, Christ whispered in my right ear: "Tell the ambulance crew to stay here. Do a stat EKG heart tracing." So before I even asked her a lot of questions, I ordered a stat EKG. When I looked at it, she had one of the worst-looking EKGs that anyone can have! Her wave patterns looked like a row of old tombstones, indicating a massive heart attack in progress. At that point, I had about ninety minutes to get her cardiac help. Fortunately, the ambulance crew did stay and we started treating her for an acute myocardial infarction. She was subsequently transferred to another regional hospital where she had an immediate heart catheterization. She did very well afterward and had no further complications. My nursing staff and the ambulance crew were initially critical of me for ordering the heart tracing, as they saw no clinical reason for it. But again, Christ had told me differently, and by following his advice, we were able to save this lady's life.

Spiritual vision

In addition to feeling Christ's presence and hearing his voice, the third spiritual sense that I developed is what I call "Christ vision." I began seeing through His eyes instead of just my human eyes.

I see the ordinary physical world quite clearly. However, with Christ's vision I also see a separate, duplicate image in my mind above my human vision. It's like looking at a movie that's being projected by two projectors at once. The alternative vision shows me auras around people or their hearts, and sometimes the cause of their medical problems. Occasionally I see the gold/white sparkle of energy which makes up all things in this world. People who tended to be more spiritual in nature had clear to pure white auras, while those who were more egotistical in nature had very gray to darker auras. The majority of people have grayish white auras.

I learned also that people's auras change, depending on a variety of factors. Fatigue, the surrounding environment, and state of mind all affect their auras.

My X-ray Vision

In addition to seeing auras, I was starting to see through

my patients bodies as if I had x-ray vision. I both saw and knew what their problem was at the same time.

An elderly patient was brought in by her family by wheelchair for evaluation of pain in her left knee, of two days duration. She had severe dementia so she could not answer questions. According to the family no trauma was involved. As I touched her and looked at her knee, there were no obvious deformities or skin changes. But then Christ showed me with His vision that the upper femur bone was broken. This fracture was apparent on her x-ray.

Another woman came in with left shoulder pain after a fall. When I looked at her left shoulder and left arm, I saw the black line of a spiral fracture near the top of her humerus bone. This was again confirmed on x-ray. As everything was in good alignment, she was treated conservatively, sent home, and did well.

Christ in the ER

An 80-year-old woman was brought into the emergency room in full cardiac arrest, with CPR in progress. We continued the cardiac code for another twenty minutes, but during this entire time, she had a flat line heart rhythm. At that point, I called the code and we stopped CPR. I pronounced her dead and everyone left the room. I was now alone with this lady.

It has always been my habit to pray for my patients when they pass away. I consider it my last service as a doctor to help my patients go home. I grew up Catholic so my prayer was usually, "Our father who art in heaven hallowed be thy name..." As I held her left hand to my chest with both of my hands, a new thought occurred to me. What if I ask Christ to take this lady home to God? Will Christ come?

So I calmed my mind and asked Christ to come and take this woman home to God for me. I asked that she be freed of the constraints of this materialistic world. In that instant, the entire room appeared in different densities of white light; I could see the energy that was in everything. The air was a very light white, while the equipment was a dense white light. All the forms were there, but I could see the energy in them for a while. Time seemed to stop, no sound was heard, and I felt a deep sense of peace envelop me. Christ appeared as a beautiful red aura in the shape of a bead across the gurney from me on my left side. My patient had a lovely white aura. She slowly sat up and for a moment, I could clearly see her face as she turned to say thank you to me. Christ picked her up and they melded together opposite me. Then, they moved together into a different dimension and floated up to the right hand side of the room. There, I saw golden doors open and a bright light filled the room. I saw the arms of God embrace both of them and draw them into heaven. I felt tremendous peace, love and joy. As I looked around, everything in the room was still dancing in scintillating white light. I realized that I had just assisted in giving someone birth into Heaven. I was awestruck. This did not last long as another emergency was on its way in and required my immediate attention. But I know this lady went home.

When I came home that night, I reflected on what had happened. I have prayed for people when they pass away for over fifteen years. Never had I seen anything like this. It was then that I remembered from the Course that death is not real but an illusion. That day I experienced this truth first hand for myself.

What I did not know is that this scenario was going to be repeated throughout the rest of my medical career. This new prayer is the one that I now use whenever someone is going to pass away or has already passed away. Whenever I ask Christ to take someone home, he always comes and guides the loved one home, if that is their wish. And I get to see this; it is such a lovely vision to behold.

A two-year-old child was brought into the ER having respiratory problems. Another provider had already ordered a chest x-ray but as he was busy, he asked if I wouldn't mind seeing this child for him. I was told by the mother that her child had been running a fever and was coughing all day. When I saw him, the infant child was straddling his mom's left leg and wearing only diapers. The mother was sheet white with terror. The child was obviously in severe respiratory distress and working very hard to breathe. Just then, the x-ray came up on the computer and I saw the child had bilateral pneumonia. I turned to examine the child but in that moment, the child leaned forward on his mother's chest, became unresponsive and stopped breathing. He had died.

Then I saw the child's white aura separate from his body and lift about three inches above it. The child's thought was: "Shall I leave this world?" Then Christ appeared on my right side as a red aura, and He was also behind the child. He said to me, "Place your hand on the baby's back." After I did this, Christ said to the child, "Stay, little one." I then witnessed the child's aura merge back with his body and as I rubbed his back, the child started breathing again. I called a pediatric code blue and we were able to fully resuscitate and stabilize the child.

Laughter with Christ

I have a bad habit of teasing my patients when they are starting to feel little bit better. Laughter is wonderful medicine for releasing someone from anxiety and fear. You cannot be anxious and fearful and be laughing at the same time. It's just not possible. Suddenly, my patient's problems do not seem so serious anymore if the doctor is joking about it. As they start to laugh with me about their medical problem, they relax. But in reality, Christ loves laughter and it is truly He and not I that is causing this mischief. I'm not guilty!

A man came in by ambulance. He was involved in a motor vehicle accident and had sustained trauma to his right foot. It was dislocated and angulated towards the right side of his body. I gave him some pain medicines and x-rayed his foot. As I looked at the x-ray of his foot, it was clear there were no obvious fractures, but rather a simple dislocation. I told him I would only give him a "B" for his injury; since his ankle wasn't broken and there was no bone showing through the skin, that was the best I could do. But I told him that he was welcome to go out and crash another car, then maybe he would get an "A" but only if he had bones protruding through his skin. He broke out laughing and said he was quite happy to have the "B." I reset his foot and told him that his procedure was easier than I expected and that he would be healed within two weeks.

A little old lady came in with a broken hip, surrounded by family, asking me why it had happened. My answer was: "You stepped in a Bangor sinkhole." You can't see them, I explained, since they're invisible and move around, but they have a propensity for finding little old ladies and breaking their hips. You have to be very careful when walking around Bangor!

While the family laughed, my patient took me seriously for a moment, moaning "Oh dear." When I told her I was teasing, the spell of fear was broken and everyone relaxed.

Spiritual confidentiality

I made it a habit to never discuss with anyone what I was seeing or feeling inwardly, as by definition I could easily be diagnosed with schizophrenia. That would not be good for my medical career or my resume.

A middle-aged man came in complaining of acute onset of chest pain, appearing anxious and uncomfortable. I ordered some medications and an electrocardiogram. As I stood on the right side of his bed reading his EKG, Christ was on my right side and looking at it with me. Silently I asked Christ, "How does this look to you?" I thought it looked fine and saw nothing acute. Christ agreed with me.

Meanwhile, the patient asked me what I thought of the heart tracing. I did not want to tell him that I was consulting with Christ about it. Though I did not see any evidence of a heart problem, I suspect he might have had one if I would have told him about my invisible consultant.

Christ recommended a G.I. "cocktail," as the patient probably had a spasm around his stomach causing him pain. This is a mixture of three medications to relieve esophageal spasm, also known as a "nutcracker esophagus" and acid indigestion. These are common causes of heart pain and mimic it. This mixture consists of Lidocaine to numb the gastrointestinal tract, Maalox to neutralize stomach acid, and finally Bentyl, a smooth muscle relaxer for the intestines. I gave him this combination of medicines this and he had immediate relief of his pain. His bloodwork was all normal and he was eventually sent home in stable condition, quite relieved.

Don't be afraid

Once you've begun a mystical journey, don't go back, don't be afraid, and don't give up. The changes that you will experience are natural and are all part of your growth process towards illumination. As soon as you allow Christ to touch your soul, you are on the path of your resurrection. Ascend with Him above your limited ego consciousness. Your ego will begin to slowly die, a little each day, and you will be reborn into the new consciousness of God. This is the whole secret of our spiritual life: the acknowledgment of our Christ consciousness within as our individual being, our True Identity.

As you learn to remove your ego's veils blocking your divine light, you will become more brilliant and radiant. As a result of this illumination, you will see and hear much farther than you can with your limited human senses. Everything will become much clearer to you as well. As the darkness decreases, your peace increases; you are becoming free. Christ will never push you farther than you can handle; from my personal experience, He knows when to let me rest and when to push.

"Fear not that you will be abruptly lifted up and hurled into reality," the Course reassures us. And then Christ says, "God willed he waken gently and with joy, and gave him means to awaken without fear." [ACIM T – 16.VI.8:1; T-27. VII.13:5] Therefore we do not go straight from nightmares to reality, but rather move through several intermediate steps, which ACIM calls the happy or gentle dreams, until we remember who we are. The realization that this world we live in, that looks so real to us, is merely a dream within our mind was incomprehensible to me at first. However, over the next ten years, I would learn to unlearn this dream and remember who I really am as an extension of God.

Over the course of several years, while seeing patients in the ER, I noticed a change in myself. My perception of the reality of any patient's problem changed. When I looked into their eyes, I could see a light within them. I was no longer distracted by the form that their illness took, no matter how severe it appeared to be. Because of this, I was calm and this calmness radiated to my patients. Within a short amount of time, everyone was at ease, smiling and sometimes laughing. I always considered my ER visit to be successful when everyone left in peace.

But what I was really starting to learn was that since I felt peaceful, confident and calm, I was able to step aside and remain centered in peace. Christ was then able to work through me, expressing His healing love to those around me. By allowing Christ's thoughts to flow through me, I learned that I could help facilitate healing in my patients. I also learned that by not reacting to the form of the illness, and treating it with some levity, my patients would relax. I would follow this levity with reassurances that their illness wasn't as bad as I initially thought, and that they would recover rather quickly. But even as I said these words, it was not me talking but rather Christ talking through me.

I learned to experience Oneness with my patients and know that they would be fine. I could feel God's Grace flowing through me to them, and experience their gratitude afterwards. They were at peace, meaning they could relax into Love's presence.

If I did become upset or distracted by the forms and temptations of the problems around me, I could not hear Christ nor feel his presence. I was off balance and felt alone. When this happened, I would reach into my pocket and touch the 4 x 6 ACIM note card on which I had written the daily lesson. As I touched this card, I would start to calm down. I was able to slow down my breathing and then re-center myself on Christ's presence. The more I practiced peace and non-reactivity, the more Christ's peace prevailed in my life.

These patient examples are just a few from my ER time. Christ is always available to us if we remain calm and centered in the now, the present time. It is such a wonderful feeling to know that we are never alone, and that with practice we can learn to develop our spiritual senses of hearing and seeing and communicating with Christ.

With time, we can all become able to communicate with Him. I have learned to relax and trust Him and in so doing, many people benefited from His love.

Be at Peace

Be at peace this day, my child, as you travel through the turnstiles of your life, for I am here to hold your hand and clear the way.

Be at peace this day, my child, for I created you in love and will therefore never leave you.

Be at peace this day, my child, for you are forever safe in my loving arms, protected at all times by my strength.

Be at peace this day, my child, my innocent child. You who could never sin or offend me in any way, let your fears return to the nothingness from where they came.

Be at peace this day, my child, be still for a while and rest. All is well. I am here to comfort you and surround you with my healing love.

Be at peace this day, my child, for wherever you travel I will walk beside you and make the crooked places straight and keep you safe.

Be at peace this day, my child, because forever we are One in Love.

Be at peace this day, my holy child.

CHAPTER 5

Galaxy Walks

During the first phase of Illumination, my meditations started to change as I learned to focus my mind. As a result, my awareness began expanding into a new and infinite spiritual dimension that I had never visited before. My astral travel resumed, now taking me well beyond the dimensions of this galaxy. Eventually, I became a pure thought of consciousness and could see everything all around me. Like my astral travels in childhood, I still could not hear anything nor feel anything. I did however retain my concepts of Rod, or my little "self".

Meditation

The sole purpose of meditation is to learn to quiet your mind's chatter so that you may enter into His presence and become One again.

Before meditating, I liked to have a cup of coffee and read something spiritual first, to help quiet my mind and focus my attention. Sometimes I would eat one granola bar if I felt really hungry. Once focused and awake, I would do some stretching exercises for a few minutes until I felt limbered up. When ready, I settled into my upright recliner chair and wrapped myself in a blanket, as I tend to get quite cold when I meditate.

I would close my eyes and start slowing my breathing down, letting my mind center itself. It takes about twenty minutes for my breathing and my body to slow down. With practice, I learned to sit and meditate for one to two hours when I had the available time. Sundays were my favorite day, as nobody wanted anything from me.

Over the next several years my mind became more quiet and centered. The endless mind chatter started to settle down the more I chose to ignore those thoughts. I thought of them as shooting stars in my mind, without reacting to any of them, just watching them go by. When I thought about why I had all the chatter, I remembered that the human brain's function is to constantly generate electrical signals that maintain our body. Some of these electrical signals are related to memory and are of no other consequence. So I decided not to fight what my brain was intrinsically designed to do.

I continued to read A Course in Miracles, then A Way of Mastery, and next A Course in Love. I also read a variety of other authors' works over the next ten years, which helped me to question the reality of this world. While reading, I could feel Christ's presence on my right side, tutoring me as certain words and phrases would go deep into my consciousness. This had the effect of freeing my mind, and as the Course suggests, "We are unlearning the world" through a process of mind training. I also went on occasional retreats to spend as much time learning as I could.

As nice as my meditations were, they were still limiting. Yes, I had a nice experience of quiet and peace, but there was no fullness to them, as I will talk about later.

I was fortunate to have met a dear friend, Tracy Pozzy,

who was trained in meditation and breathwork. With her help, I started to have out-of-body experiences again, and with practice I was very comfortable and felt safe and secure. I felt invulnerable.

At first, I needed Tracy's help and guidance in order to travel. She would place her hands around my head as I lay on a mattress covered with blankets. I would start breathing as she spoke gently to me. She helped me learn how to control my breathing and remove my blocks to love's presence. Though my body lay on the mattress, I became disconnected from it. A part of me became light and started to float.

Initially, I would stay several inches above my body and not really go anywhere, getting used to the sensation of being light. I sensed a white outline of my body at first, but then this changed into more of an amorphous shape, and with time I was left only with a clear thought of awareness.

After perhaps after a year of working with Tracy, one day I floated out of her home and went into a deep, mountainous forest. I remember looking at a fallen tree and seeing all the life and energy that was still within it. I saw the mold, the cells of the tree, its bark, the ferns and grass surrounding it, as well as the surrounding trees. My vision spanned 360° and everything I saw was clearer than my ordinary physical vision could possibly be. I could see life flowing through everything and I was one with it.

As my mind continued to expand, I started to travel around the earth, like being in a jet aircraft flying at supersonic speed. I saw lakes, mountains, cities, and clouds below me. It was so easy to encircle the earth at a breathtaking pace. I felt absolutely nothing in terms of cold or wind, and I heard no noise. I had no discomfort of any kind, only the absolute awareness of total freedom. This was truly a beautiful state to be in.

But I did not settle for just traveling around the earth. I wanted to go farther. Once I made this decision, I left the earth behind. I had a glimpse of the moon on one occasion. As I traveled deeper into space, I could clearly see the canopy of stars all around me but I did not know my ultimate destination.

As my travels progressed, I had a brief episode of first being outside the Sun, and then I went deep into the heart of it. Again I felt no discomfort or sensation of any kind. I was able to watch individual atoms collide and give off clear energy that I suppose scientists would describe as plasma. There was a variety of colors swirling around, consisting of red, orange, yellow and white. It seemed to me that as all these colors mixed and collided, the same clear energy was given off. It was amazing to see this reaction.

Next, what really caught my attention once was Jupiter. I saw the bright orange oval on the lower part of the planet as well several dark bands encircling it. Jupiter appeared to be a ball about four feet across and my awareness was several times this size. Again there was the backdrop of stars and space. I kept moving outward and away from the sun.

With time, my mind continued to expand in size as I traveled through the galaxy, and eventually I found myself looking down on our own Milky Way. I could clearly see its center as a white sphere of light, as well as the two arms, and a multitude of stars above and below. I saw galaxies everywhere that I looked, and I knew that we are certainly not alone in this dimension. I felt peaceful and content, knowing that I was going to be okay and perfectly safe.

It was here, while looking at the galaxies, that I had another experience of seeing Christ. He appeared to me as a translucent white human form wearing a robe. He stood opposite me on one end of a small, grassy green field, with the canopy of galaxies in space surrounding us. The field was surrounded by a short white picket fence with no gates. Christ just looked at me, neither speaking nor moving. I tried talking with Him but He just stared at me with a slight smile on his face. This experience repeated a number of times, and was always the same. Eventually I noticed that the fenced area seemed to be holding me back, and then I wanted to move beyond it and continue with my journey. Then one day Christ, the grass, and the fence were gone. I was free to travel again.

As my mind continued to expand even more, I came to a place where the galaxies ended. It was as if they were being held back by a sheet of glass below me and extending through the universe. All the galaxies existed below this division, and above this plane of glass there was an area of space that I call "Twilight." There are no stars here, only a deep violet color. Once I passed through this sheet of glass, I could float along effortlessly and look down at all the galaxies below me. I had no sensations of anything except a deep peace and contentment. I took this journey many times, and afterward when I woke up, the feeling of peace persisted throughout the day. I also noticed how limiting this body and this world were to me. Something was always demanding my attention and I just wanted to let it all go.

On one of my trips, a profound event changed my life. As usual, I was enjoying my travels through the Twilight when I came to the edge of it. I could see the sheet of glass below me, bending 90° downward. I had the impression of standing on the edge of this sheet of glass, looking down, and all I could see were roiling dark clouds of turbulence below me. When I looked in front of me I saw a curtain of clouds falling down into an abyss. The distance across was too far to jump, and I did not know what was on the other side as I could not see through the clouds. I knew that if I fell into the abyss I would die. But something inside of me was pulling me to go forward and I knew I had to trust that I would be okay.

In that moment, I decided that I wanted to proceed, try to jump the distance and hope for the best. In that instant, Christ reached through the cloud curtain and I could clearly see his outline as a perfectly pure white human being with outstretched arms. He was reaching out to catch me. I did not have to do this alone! I knew I was going to make it, and felt so happy to know that he was going to catch me and help me across. So I jumped into his arms and he pulled me through a very thin veil of curtains into the vast infinity of Heaven.

The Curtains in my life

As I traveled along the road of my life journey, I came to a dark black curtain covering the sky and obscuring everything in front of me. As I approached it, I became afraid for I did not know what it hid from me. What was so horrible in my life that it had to be covered up? I gently parted the curtain and saw only darkness. I felt the chill and fear of death on my back so I quickly let the curtain go. As I backed away, my fear diminished. Clearly, the right thing to do was turn around and go back the way I had come. At least I knew this way from past experience.

As I journeyed back, everything was fine until I met Christ coming towards me. He asked me where I'd been, and why I was walking back. I explained to him about the curtain of death that I was too afraid to go. He smiled at me and said, "Let me come with you for I have a lantern that will help light your way. Then you will be able to see through the curtain to the other side. But, I will only do this if you want me to help you. I will also walk slightly in front of you so you can see beyond your steps better."

I agreed to His help and thanked Him for it. So, we turned around and started to walk forward again on the road towards the black curtain.

As we approached it, I became afraid again. Realizing this, Christ took my hand and I was comforted. At the curtain, He asked me to part it for him. Trusting Him, I did so and He lifted the lantern high, casting light through the opening so I could see the other side. There was another road, trees, mountains and lakes. But it all looked so different and inviting, fresh and new. So together, we stepped through this black curtain of death and, laughing at my fears, we continued walking onward.

As we journeyed on, I came to more dark curtains and we repeated the process of opening them, walking through them and laughing. I noticed that I was getting lighter, that the curtains were becoming thinner, like veils that I could almost see though, and the land was starting to sparkle with white light. Christ never let go of my hand and kept his lantern ready.

I came to one curtain unlike the others, for it was golden white. I felt no fear and only peace. "What curtain is this?" I asked, and Christ said, "It is your last one." I asked him if he was going to leave me now and he said, "No, I will never leave you, but here you will be safe so go ahead and open it."

As I parted the curtain, God stepped through, picked me up and held me in his arms. He kissed me and said, "Welcome home my child, I have missed you. Please come in."

As I looked at Christ, I realized He was my guide and my brother who helped me find my way home through the land of curtains. I said, "Thank you brother."

He just smiled and laughed, then walked with me into our Father's house.

CHAPTER 6

The Unreality of Death

In November 2011, I retired from the ER and became the medical director for several nursing homes in the Bangor, Maine region. After a few years, I also became the medical director for Beacon Hospice. My medical practice changed from an acute care setting to end-of-life care, where dying people are looked after on a day-to-day basis. As a result, their transition from this world is gradual and the families have time to adjust. Patients in this environment usually die because their bodies just wear out.

I personally witnessed the transition or death of several hundred people. Since I was able to see with the vision of Christ, I could see Christ and a patient's aura join together. I learned from all these transitions that we never truly die. We merely change from the form of a human body to existing as clear light in a formless spiritual dimension.

As I changed my career path, I was also entering the second phase of my life's learning as a mystic. I call this the "Atonement Phase." I was meditating daily and reading spiritual literature, becoming very calm and peaceful within and learning to extend this peace to those around me. My thoughts of judgment and projection were greatly diminished as I became capable of just letting life flow. I knew exactly what to do beyond a shadow of a doubt, because Christ was my guide.

During the next five years, as I said, I would help several hundred people leave this world with the help of Christ and be reborn into Heaven. I call this process "Giving Birth into Heaven."

As my patients approached the end of their life, Christ always came, and with time I didn't even have to ask for him; he just showed up. When he did, a frame shift would occur and my heart would open up. God's love would then flow through me to everyone around. When love flows like this, no matter what the circumstances are, I call this Grace. Everybody becomes calm and peaceful because their heart resonates with God's "Amazing Grace."

What I find so deeply moving and beautiful to watch is a person's white aura depart, literally leaving their bodily baggage behind. They let go of their ego world and merge with Christ. From there, Christ takes them home to Heaven and for just a moment, I see the arms of God reach through these doors and pull a loved one back inside. They have gone back home, never to return to this dream-land of the ego and separation from God again.

In this chapter, I'll share a few of my experiences in helping people transition to their divine essence of light, love and peace.

The Physiology of Death

When someone is beginning their dying process, they go through several stages. By knowing about the stages, I am able to give a reasonable estimate of the time of passing to the patient or family. I am always amazed at how strong and resilient the human body is; sometimes people don't follow my estimating rules, and this makes me look bad! Here are the guidelines that I use nonetheless.

First, when a person stops eating they will usually pass away in about four weeks, depending on their muscle mass and fat mass. Without food, the body burns both fat and muscle protein. I always look at a person's arms and legs and measure the circumference of these two areas. As muscle is burned for fuel, the circumference of the limb decreases. People usually look quite gaunt at the end of their life and it's because the body was trying to stay alive by burning muscle and fat as fuel.

The second phase is when a person stops drinking water or liquids. The body needs water to flush poison out of itself. Without the intake of fluids, death usually occurs within a few days to a week.

The third phase is when acid starts to build up in the body. This phase is called "ketoacidosis." Since the body cannot excrete acid through the kidneys and urine, the acid is blown off by breathing. Usually, this acid has a sweet smell, like nail polish remover. When I notice this, the patient is usually unresponsive and death will occur within three days.

When I did Intensive Care Medicine, sometimes I would do an Electroencephalogram or EEG during this phase of dehydration and ketoacidosis, checking for any brainwave activity. Usually there was none so I knew that the conscious part of the person's mind was gone and the body was just using up the last of its fuel. This is like stepping out of your car with the engine running, letting it run down until there is no more fuel left.

During this phase, I also knew the patient felt no pain. I would push on the base of their fingernail plate to see if they would withdraw from pain, which would be an indication of consciousness. If I could press pretty hard without the finger being withdrawn, the patient was completely unconscious.

Abnormal Behaviors

During the dying process, at any point some people can become very confused, anxious or agitated. This is not a reflection of them as a person, but merely indicates that their brain circuitry is not working properly. I use medication to help soothe the circuits and induce calm, as angry or abusive behavior is very hard on the patient, the family, and staff. Seizures may also occur, but can likewise be managed with medication.

Sometimes patients will have what are called hemi-ballistic movements. An arm will shoot up into the air, the patient will sit up abruptly, or otherwise start moving in an abnormal manner. This too is very upsetting to the family because they interpret it as painful, but this is not the case. Again, the cause is a short circuit within the brain that can be easily treated.

In the final phases of a person's life, breathing becomes irregular and erratic. There are occasional pauses or gasps that will get longer and longer. After the last breath there will be a few more heartbeats, and then the heart stops.

As a hospice doctor, I would always use a low dose of medicines to keep my patients comfortable. I tried to keep them conscious and comfortable for as long as possible. But during the last three days, they would just rest comfortably. During this time, they would fall into a deep sleep, and a few days later they would simply leave their body behind.

What is it Like to Die?

I met Anna when she was nearing the end of her life. She was 73 and had stage 4 pancreatic cancer; her last therapy had failed and thereafter she requested that I admit her to my Hospice service. She was a kind and pleasant woman who had led a simple life. As I finished admitting her to our Hospice service, she asked me, "What is it like to die?"

I told her about the dying process and the medications that I would use to usher her into a very restful sleep, to be followed a few days later by her body ceasing to function. I said, "You will never know it. As you drift off, you will feel an incredible lightness of being. You will float some as you disconnect from your body. You will be very peaceful, and I will make sure that you do not suffer any pain or fear."

Anna looked at me as I was talking, while her daughter cried softly. I felt a very deep connection to her. Then Anna had a beautiful smile on her face and she said, "Now I see you." I hugged her and kissed her cheek. "You promised me peace and now I have it. Thank you." I could see that she was at peace.

Over the next few weeks, I would visit Anna to see how she was doing. She was always happy and peaceful, and had had no fear and no pain. She had several lucid times and visited with her family and friends. During this transition time, Anna was alert for a while and then would sleep. She was still able to eat and drink water. Her friends would visit and they would enjoy each other's company. In the last week of her life, I saw Christ standing on the right side of Anna's bed as a red aura. He radiated love, peace and contentment. He was patiently waiting for Anna to let go of her body so he could help guide her home.

During this time, Anna's daughter placed a vase of variegated red and white tulips on a table in the same place where Christ stood. They were a symbol to me of Christ's presence and love for us. The petal's white tips were for Anna and the petal's red base was Christ. There was no sharp line between the two colors but rather they were interlaced at their union. The flowers themselves were all closed.

Anna passed away on a sunny Saturday afternoon. She had been unresponsive for several days beforehand, but had awakened Friday morning and was lucid for two hours. She said good bye to her family and friends, then she fell asleep never to wake again. During this time, the family told me that the tulips all opened up.

I was at home when Anna's family called me that Saturday. I consoled the family and said I would come over shortly. After I hung up, I raised my arms up and I asked Christ to take Anna home for me. Immediately, I saw Anna's pure white aura enter my dining room on my left. Her face was perfectly clear and peaceful; she was radiant in light and joy. This vision was superimposed on my human vision. As she went by, she blew me a kiss. On her left side, there was the red aura of Christ holding her and guiding her home. I saw a few white globes float along as well, crossing my visual field from left to right, and then they were gone. I was filled with such joy and love that I cried. There was no sadness. I had just witnessed Anna's birth into Heaven. There is such love and beauty to behold at this time in one's life, and for a split second, I get to see Heaven. I was filled with gratitude to be a part of Anna's birth and to be touched by God's grace.

Then I went to Anna's home and viewed her body. She

looked so relaxed and content. Everyone felt sad but at the same time they were at peace. I held each person for a while and let them cry, feeling deep love and compassion for each one. This love radiated from God through me to them, and as they felt this love, they started to know that everything was fine. They relaxed into love's presence.

Anna is home now with God, never to return to this dream. She returned to what He created her as in Heaven: His Holy Child. They are together, once again, in perfect Love.

Before she died, Anna asked me a second question. "I do not believe in God," she said. "What will happen to me?"

I answered, "As you enter your final days of your life, Christ will be here for you, to take you home so you do not get lost along the way. In the meantime, you are going to start to remember that you are a thought of love in the mind of God, still one with Him in Heaven. Love is your true essence. God is not found in churches and religion, but only in your heart where you feel love."

As I explained this to Anna, a variety of white orbs filled the space above her bed. They floated above her as thoughts of love — angels who came to help her be at peace and find her way home. They were beautiful to see.

Anna had asked me to preside over her funeral. A few days later during a morning meditation, Anna told me what it's like to walk with angels.

Angels Walk Here

As I enter into deep meditation, a warm blanket of peace covers my mind and all is quiet within me. I can now hear the voice of God calling me home. As I walk towards this loving voice, I start to see the dawn of Heaven in the horizon of my thoughts. With joy in my heart, I come to the doorway of Heaven. With only a breath, I cross over the threshold into the eternal light of Love. I am now free of my body and my thoughts of separation. Angels walk here and I am now one, as a thought of love, one with all of my brothers and all that I see. Into this vastness of light and love, God welcomes me home and gently embraces all of us as one. I am no longer blind but can see with the light of Christ that my dreams were nothing and I will soon forget them. I am awake now, in this holy instant remembering my true home. Eternally safe and at peace. I am at home walking with angels in the light of our Father's love.

I invite you up here to walk with me in this light, here with angels and here, with God. Still your restless mind, close your eyes and listen for God's gentle voice calling you home. The way is as easy as your breathing. Relax and let it flow. You too will be guided home into our Father's loving arms and His loving heart.

Peace, be still and know that we are all one in His eternal light of love and at home, here, where angels walk.

My Dad the Atheist

My dad was an atheist who complained to me about God, churches, and cemeteries, as well as all the wars, crimes, and hatred in this world. "If God was so loving, why is he allowing all of these atrocities to happen?" he would challenge me. "Why is God so fickle, both loving one minute and then wrathful the next? This does not sound like a loving God to me!"

Yet Dad gave love, support and money to those he cared

about and to those he did not. He offered friendship and guidance to all who sought his help, and was very generous and kind.

He was 87 when I could see in his eyes that his life was ending. He finally told me one day, "I am all done." From that day on, he started to let go of everything that he held dear. I helped him get admitted to a private hospice organization and I stayed with him for the last week of his life.

Four days before he left his body, Christ appeared as a red aura on Dad's right side, holding his spirit in peace and love. I felt such kindness and gentleness and I was thankful for his presence. Dad was deeply comfortable now in body and spirit.

In those final days of his life here, I also saw several white auras on his left side. They were of different sizes and I did not know who they represented at first, but then I recognized the tallest one as Uncle Vernon. In a family of seven, Dad was the last one alive. Now I saw that his whole family was here to help him with his transition into his new life.

Two days before he left us, I saw the golden gates of Heaven open wide for him. Christ was there as well as Dad's family. All was set for him, but he still was not ready to leave. I was guided to read passages from A Course in Miracles about God's love for us and about how despite our mistakes and misconceptions about Him, God saw only love in us. I could feel my father start to understand, relax, and realize that perhaps he'd been wrong about God — and that was okay.

On the day before Dad left, I walked into his room in the morning. His spirit, Christ, and his family were all gone. Where did they go? I also noticed that the gates of heaven were no longer visible to me. I concluded that Dad's body was just idling on what little fuel was left, so I stayed for the day just holding him, kissing him and loving him.

On the next day, when I returned from lunch, it appeared that Dad had taken his last breath. I tapped his chest and said, "Have you left us?" I saw the last two pulsations of blood flow in his neck, then stop. My father had waited until everyone left the room to pass away, a very common occurrence. This passage seems to be a very private time for the dying. I lifted Dad's right hand to my heart and cried from the depth of my being for the loss I felt. Eventually I felt the warmth of Christ's peace upon me and I released my father.

As a final goodbye, I walked to the head of his bed and read ACIM's Workbook Lesson 109, "I rest in God," to everyone in the room. As I began, the room went quiet and peace descended upon us. Standing on my right was the bright white aura of my dad, outlined in gold. He sparkled with happiness and love; I had never seen him so clearly. He glowed with the love that he'd found within, My heart glowed with love as well, and my sorrow vanished. He was not his body anymore but the Holy Child of God, present to say his last goodbye. As I finished reading the lesson, he vanished. But I still felt the joy of his presence upon my heart. My dad the atheist went home to his Father.

God was unlike anything that Dad was taught. All his doubts and fears dissolved in God's love for him and in that instant, the atheist smiled. He became one with Love again. The atheist radiated his love to me and then said good-bye. It did not matter what his beliefs were or what he did in his life; God did not care. My dad, the atheist, went home. But before he left, he gave me a message that I will share with you now.

Dad's Goodbye, June 8, 2015

To my beloved family and friends, I thank you for your love and support as I have entered the twilight of my life. My body, which has served me well for so long, is tired now and needs to rest. In this time of transition, I am finally free of pain and feel a deep sense of peace growing within. There is a freedom and lightness of being that I have never felt before.

It is joyful for me to hear your music and voices, even though you think I am asleep. Though I can no longer respond, I feel your touch and am comforted.

Soon my body will cease to exist. But I find that I am becoming free as a spirit of love. As I lift out of this body, I open up beautiful white wings and start to soar into the heavens above. But I am not alone. There are angels here who have come and are helping me learn to fly, and Christ Himself is guiding me home.

My pain and suffering are fading like a bad dream as I feel a profound sense of peace and joy. I am giddy with this new sensation. And oh, I can see. I CAN SEE! The doorways of Heaven are open wide and God himself is there with open arms, smiling to me, welcoming me home. Soon I will be in His arms, one with Love again.

I see all of you around here with me, and I see your grief, pain and suffering. It need not be. For I am here in your hearts and memories, forever with you. I will still be here for you and though you will not see me as a body, I will touch your hearts and you will feel me there. I have loved you always, my family and friends, and that will never change. Be still and feel my presence, feel my love. I am not gone, just different now. Relax and know how much I love and cherish you.

I am thankful to all of you who entered my life. You taught me much about loving, caring and giving. I have learned compassion, and as a result I have felt Grace. I am a better person because of you, and for that I am indeed forever grateful.

It is time for me to leave this body now. Let me go. It is okay. Relax and be at peace, for all is well. I am only going home and returning to the Love from which we are all born. I will be here with God, waiting for you when you to are ready to come home. I love you all and for now, I temporarily say good bye. — RODNEY D. CHELBERG, SR.

"Will God forgive me?"

Betty had end-stage lung disease and decided to stay home with her family where she felt. Nonetheless I sensed resistance and fear in Betty as I sat next to her bed and held her hand. I asked her what she was afraid of. She asked me, "Am I good enough for God? Do you think God still wants me, and will He will forgive me even though I have made so many mistakes?"

I spoke to her of who she truly was: an independent expression of divinity, a true child of God. It seems the world is devoted to teaching us this is not so, and thus we should fear both death and God. In fact, these ideas are false, for we are forever connected to God and we need only to relax into His presence. He is waiting for us with open arms. So I told Betty to rest easy, explaining that she had done nothing wrong and that she could never offend God, no matter what the world says. I could feel Christ talking through me to her:

To my child: I see you always as innocence, an extension

of me and my love for you. You see yourself as a shadow, filled with doubt, lack and fear, separated from me and lost to a world of time and space. You feel isolated, alone and cold. You feel guilty for leaving me, and afraid that I will seek retribution. Yet these are merely fears based on nothing.

Take heart. Feel your heart beating, pumping life to your brain and body. It is doing this not to nourish you now, but to give you time to change your mind and remember that no matter what you do, your heart, like my love, keeps beating.

I see you as light, free of all doubt, lack and fear. You have only dreamed of pain and death in fantasies. In Truth, you are golden white, a divine light. I see you as Holy, forever free and innocent in this light of Truth. Come to hear my words and take them to your heart. Believe me when I say, "You are my child in whom I am well pleased."

As the darkness of your mind's fear is washed away by your forgiving thoughts, truth is reflected back to you and you will see your light of innocence. Then your Christ light will start to shine in your life. Let me help you remember who you are.

Betty heard this message from Him and became convinced of her innocence. Then she was able to relax. One week later, she had a very peaceful passing. Her daughters stated that she appeared very comfortable, and just fell asleep.

The passing of an alcoholic

Roger was admitted to hospice because he was dying from end-stage liver disease stemming from chronic alcohol abuse. His had been a traumatic life, and he self-medicated with drinking to keep his demons at bay. Over time the alcohol had changed his personality, and Roger had become quite abusive, leading to estrangement from his wife and his children.

One winter evening, I was visiting with Roger and his wife. He was filled with anger and I knew that if Roger could not forgive his past, then he would be trapped and have to relive his life again. Roger also felt very guilty about the abusive acts he had perpetrated on his family. He confessed that he couldn't stop thinking, "What have you done with all the love that God has given you?"

So with his wife present, I held Roger's hands and looked into his eyes and asked him to repeat after me: "I, Roger, forgive those in my past and I forgive myself."

It took many tries for Roger to say this, but suddenly his ego's wall broke down and he started crying. His wife started crying as well. Love's presence had broken through the wall that was within his mind and washed him clean. His wife then joined in holding our hands together and in that moment, God spoke through me to Roger and his wife. Here is what God said to Roger:

Roger's Prayer

"Out of Love you were born, free to create and explore this life, and now it is time to return to Spirit, to Love and to Peace. Forever are you sinless and free of guilt, for I have loved you always. The memories of your life will end with this body and trouble you no more. Your light will shine again because you are still one with Me."

Roger relaxed and felt forgiven. His wife later recounted that he was able to let go of a lot of baggage and forgive himself, as well as those around him. He was finally at peace. She also said that he returned to the man she fell in love with when they married thirty years earlier.

Isn't this a beautiful miracle? No matter where we are on life's journey, as long as we wake up at some point, the rest does not matter. Peace has arrived. Roger had a peaceful transition several weeks later.

Roger came from light, visited here for a while and then returned to light. He was able to leave all the darkness of trauma, alcohol abuse, mistakes, judgments, and guilt behind. He let his anger go. About a year later, his son came to visit and stayed overnight in Roger's bed. He woke up and felt his father's presence in the room with him. He was nervous at first but then relaxed and as he did so, he felt loved by his dad again. They both felt peace. All was forgiven.

I too was touched by Roger's experience, helping me to remember God and recall that I too am sinless, guiltless and free. There are no shadows of doubt anymore. Roger taught me this:

God's Gifts

I lay my loving hands on you and bless you with my gifts of love, peace and joy. Feel my tenderness upon you and relax into me. Feel the warmth of my loving presence for you. Trust me as you let go. Then courage and hope will flow into your being and you will again shine as the light of the world. Your light will illuminate your life with the warmth and brightness of sunlight, extending to all the people in this world.

Let all your concerns go now and be free. Loosen your hold on this earthly life, your cares, your worries, even its joys. Unclasp your hands and relax. Put aside all thoughts of your future and of your past. As you relinquish them, your hands are free to receive my treasures as I hold them out to you in love.

Take my gifts of everlasting life, peace and joy for I give them freely. Ascend into the resurrection of your spiritual life. Then join with me now, my holy child, and we will be complete, forever as one in eternal Love. Be at peace and know that all is well.

Unexpected Death

While working in the emergency room, I had to take care of many people who died unexpectedly, from an accident, stroke, heart attack, or other causes. When people pass suddenly, there is a rip in the fabric of their life as well as their survivors' lives. Everyone is stunned because without time to prepare for a transition, people are understandably overwhelmed with grief and pain.

I never saw Christ at the bedside of these people because there was a lot of frantic activity in the emergency room when I was trying to save their lives. It was too noisy, too chaotic and too distracting. However, afterward I would sit in a small chapel that was next to the ER, or any other available quiet spot. Once my mind was quiet, I could easily find the person who had passed away. He or she would be walking along as if dazed and confused, not knowing what had happened, lost in a dimensionless reality with a gray background.

I would quietly approach and extend love to the lost spirit, trying to explain what happened and that they had left this world. But ordinarily I could not communicate with people in this in-between state. In all of these instances, Christ came, smiled at me, and started to walk with my patients and gently talk to them. He was comforting them with his presence and gently guiding them along. It's always quite beautiful and soothing to me to see someone being guided by Christ in this manner. I wished that I could show the loved ones left behind what I saw, for I knew it would bring them peace. But I was sure he would take care of them as well.

Suicide

Suicide is an especially traumatic form of sudden death, always brought about by severe pain or deep depression. Suicides are exhausted and just want their pain to stop, whatever the causes. They see no hope and have fallen into a black abyss from which they cannot escape. Suicide seems to be their only option to get away from the overwhelming discomfort they are experiencing. Their intention is never to hurt anyone and cause more sorrow and pain; they just want to end their own suffering.

Though their physical human pain is gone after dying, they still have a lot of pain within their mind. Their spiritual light is covered by a dark heavy curtain, as they still identify with their pain. I have found that I could not really talk to these people but merely observe them walking along with the background of darkness all around them.

However, in these cases, Christ seems to spend extra time walking with these spirits. He usually has his right arm over their shoulders and is gently talking to them in a gentle, kind, and supportive manner. His love is always palpable to me. Christ reassures me that that he will take good care of them and they will be fine.

Even if I found out about a suicide weeks after the fact, I could still find that person's spirit and ask Christ for help. I always felt compassion for these people who experienced a traumatic death of any kind. I also felt sadness and wished that there were more that I could do for them. I was always reassured by Christ that I had done a good job and that He would take care of my patients now. There was nothing further for me to do.

Lost

During two separate meditations, I was guided to help some people find their way home who were stuck here in this world after their sudden death.

First, I found several soldiers who were killed during the fighting that was going on all around them. Their uniforms looked like they were from World War II. I could see the remains of a brick building with only two sides standing, obviously in an active war zone. It was a clear summer day. One soldier was standing and four others were lying or sitting on the ground, all looking down. I could see their bloodied uniforms, their wounds, and the destruction of everything around them.

The one soldier who was standing came over to me and said, "We don't know how to get home. Can you help us?" After sudden deaths, they did not have time to adjust to the loss of their lives. So they were stuck in this one moment of time. I looked to the questioning soldier and pointed over my right shoulder to a light in the sky. "That is the way home," I suggested. "Look to the light and you will be guided home." He thanked me and looked at the light. In that instant, they were all gone.

In another meditation, I was guided into a house that had burned down. There was a young mother standing with her arms draped over a little boy standing in front of her. Their clothing suggested an era sometime in the 1700s. They had obviously died in the fire. She looked at me and was so sad. She said, "We don't know how to get home, will you please help us?"

So again, I had her look towards my right side and into the sky. There was a shining light that she could see. I said, "See that light, turn towards it and you will go home." As she turned and looked at the light, she and her son vanished from my sight and my meditation promptly ended.

Empty Arms

During my fourth year of medical school, before I was on my mystical path, I was called in to see a young woman who was at full-term in her pregnancy. She was in obvious pain and crying because she knew her child was dead; she felt no movement anymore. She and her husband were beside themselves with grief and pain. I delivered her stillborn baby and placed the infant on her chest for a little while. The hardest part for me was when the nurses took her stillborn baby away. I was stunned beyond belief, and I felt their tremendous loss. It was so overwhelming to me. This was among the hardest deaths that I have ever had to deal with. I gently held her and her husband in my arms for a while and we just cried.

Losing children was the most difficult event that I ever had to deal with. My mind goes absolutely blank and all I see is darkness when I experience such loss. My former wife also had a miscarriage with our first pregnancy and I could not comprehend it. All I could do was hold her in my arms. My arms felt empty and I knew she felt this, probably more so. Our arms were waiting to hold a child who was not to be.

Later in my life, once I was on my mystical path, a young woman wrote to me about her fourth miscarriage. She was beside herself with grief and pain from her multiple losses. "Where are my children?" she asked. I did not know how to answer her so I asked Christ on her behalf, "What you do when you have empty arms? Arms that should hold a child and that child is not there?" Here was Christ's reply, which I later wrote back to this young woman.

The Rose

Holy child of mine, I will not leave you comfortless and I will not forget you or those you were to meet. Give me your pain, your suffering and your loss and I will give you a red rose to be placed there in your heart. And with this rose, you will feel my constant love for you and again be whole and complete. In your arms, you will feel the gentleness of my touch and in your mind, you will have peace.

Does everyone go home?

God gave us free will and has never interfered with it, as one of His fundamental laws. During my medical career, even though I have always asked Christ to help take people home, not everyone accepts this gift.

Mr. Crocker was admitted with end stage dementia to our nursing home. He was an angry and aggressive man, abusive to his family and the facility staff. He would periodically become uncontrollable, and at one point we had to call the police and have him taken to the hospital.

When I accepted his return, I put him on some mood stabilizing medicine which helped a great deal. His family refused to come and see him anymore. When I would visit him, I could feel the anger and rage inside that his body could no longer act on.

"Fine," I could hear him say in his mind to me — "I am leaving!" I could see the light inside of him, but his aura was thick and dark. He was so identified with his anger and his body. Over the next few weeks, he stopped eating and would not get out of bed. In the last days of his life, I asked Christ to come and take him home. But this was not to be. When he died, I could see his gray aura as he stood there in the darkness of space with his arms crossed. Christ stood a few feet away on his right but could not touch him; the separation persisted. I pleaded with my patient but to no avail. "I don't want this," he said, "I am not ready." Then Mr. Crocker disappeared into nothingness. Christ stayed and told me that he would wait for Mr. Crocker and not forget him. When he is ready, Christ will bring him home for me.

I held Mr. Crocker in the light within my mind and wished him and his family peace. There was nothing else to do but let him go. Not everyone is ready to go home and we cannot force this transition on them.

My Own Death Memory

In what I call a "dream memory," I can see the following scenario very clearly within my mind. It is World War I, and I'm lying in a trench about four feet deep, muddy and wearing military combat fatigues. Above the ladders and barbed wire,

I can see a bright blue sky with white clouds floating about. All around me is the sound of screaming men, gunfire, and cannon fire. I've been shot in my left lower body and cannot move. As I lay there, another shell lands a few feet near me but does not explode immediately. As I look around me, I see my friends running away. When I turn and look at the shell again, it explodes.

In that instant, I am free, just a thought of consciousness surrounded by peace and quiet. My first thought is: "That's it?" Nothing feels hurt; the transition was instantaneous; there was no horrible experience to go through. Why had I been so afraid of death when it is, in fact, a non-event? I cannot even say that it was amazing. It was nothing. Blink, I was free.

Little Maggie

Little Maggie was my neighbor's Westie dog who loved being around me. Whenever I visited, she had to be in my lap or near me. Apparently, this was unusual behavior for her, and her owners always commented on the fact. But after several years, she passed away and I made a small urn for her ashes.

Then while I was in my kayak one clear October day, when I stopped to rest a deep feeling of peace overcame me. When I did so, a frame shift occurred and I felt connected to everything around me. The sun was off the bow of my boat and I watched the light dancing on the water. A tennis-ball-size orb of light came from the stern of my boat up to my right side. I lifted this ball of light out of the water and it stayed in my hand, glowing white with flecks of gold moving through it. I felt tremendous love and gratitude coming toward me, and I realized it was little Maggie's spirit that I was holding in my hand. I enjoyed her presence for several minutes, and then she said goodbye. I put her little spiritual presence back in the water and she returned to the stern of the boat, disappearing by the time I got to shore. I was happy to have had the chance to say goodbye to little Maggie.

Minds are joined

When someone has died and left this material plane, in spirit their mind is still present with yours. All minds are joined because there is only one mind. They have transitioned from a material form and returned to light while you are still in material form; therefore, with your limited human vision, you cannot see them. But you can still communicate by learning to shut down your five senses and becoming very still and quiet. Lose your thoughts of the departed as a human body and see them as light. Let go of conditions that may still be unresolved. Become receptive to the divine sense of Christ that is within you and them. Ask Him to help you and the other person to heal any problems if need be. Trust, let go and let God. Relax and be still. Ponder the idea that all are one in the light of God.

Do not tell God what to do. Surrender your will and listen for the voice of the Holy Spirit. Wait until you feel the presence of Christ within you as a divine presence. Once you have this feeling of love, His all-knowing mind will spring forth from your heart, find its way, and heal the very things that you need healed in your relationship. If forgiveness is needed, all will be washed clean by the Holy Spirit's solvent of love, and everyone will be left holy, pure, and innocent. The miracle of healing has occurred and peace prevails.

So be glad and joyful that even though someone is gone,

we are still able to communicate with them. I personally do not want to be an anchor to anyone's spirit, with feelings of loss and bereavement or feelings of upset and anger. That is baggage they do not need.

"...we are of one mind, and that mind is ours. See only this mind everywhere, because only this is everywhere and in everything. It is in everything because it encompasses all things within itself. Blessed are you who perceive only this because you perceive only what is true." [ACIM T-7.V.10:9-12]

The 'Reality' of Death

I no longer believe in the reality of death and do not fear it; the idea of death is meaningless to me. I know that our consciousness resides in Heaven with God and not here in this body. The body is an illusion; we are taught to believe that this is who we really are by the ego. But the body is just a projection of our mind onto an illusionary dream world.

I have seen inside every aspect of the human body and I have never found "a center of consciousness." In my experience, consciousness is found deep within my mind and still at home with God.

Also, at the moment of someone's death, a patient weighs 150 pounds and is moving. In the next minute, they have "died" and they are no longer moving, yet they still weigh 150 pounds. What has changed? They have merely let go of their mind's projection of their body and returned to Heaven.

My job is to assist them with letting go of their body, help them to leave their mental baggage behind and overcome any fear or limits that they may have of returning home to God. Once they are free of their dreams, they can return to Heaven fully awake.

Since the body was not made by God, it cannot be real. And without our consciousness supplying our beliefs and spiritual energy to it, the body will return in time to dust or to the nothingness from which it came. Everything in this world is slowly decaying back to dust and nothingness because consciousness is slowly being withdrawn from it.

"Death's worshipers may be afraid. And yet, can thoughts like these be fearful? If they saw that it is only this which they believe, they would be instantly released. And you will show them this today. There is no death, and we renounce it now in every form, for their salvation and for our own as well. God made not death. Whatever form it takes must therefore be illusion. This is the stand we take today. And it is given us to look past death, and see the life beyond." [ACIM W-163.8:1-9]

Why then are we so afraid of death? Does it bother us to turn off our car and step out? Is the body any different? We're so attached to these bodies and believe in them as our true identity. But this is not so. I wish people could see what I see: We are a divine white light, we are Christ consciousness expressing itself in this world as a limited human form. I believe that if people could see the illusion of this dream, then they would not be so afraid of leaving their body behind.

So, I consider it my last act as a doctor to give a dying patient and his or her family a blessing of love, a blessing of peace. Sometimes I'm silent, and other times I will hold my patient's hand and bring it to my heart while I pray for them and the family. Then I know that I have asked on behalf of this person to be returned home to God.

With the quietness that then settles upon the room,

everyone's mind is now starting to connect and we are now communicating at a very deep level. The ego may still be trying to prove to us that this person's death will be triumphant over God's Will. But, the gentle persuasion that comes from the Holy Spirit convinces the family that this is not so. "To you and your brother, in whose special relationship the Holy Spirit entered, is given release and being released from the dedication to death. For it was offered (them), and (they) accepted." [ACIM T-19.IV.C.1:1-2]

Since I believe that "death is only a shadow," those around me can also start to resonate with that thought and accept it. They begin to find acceptance and peace because they can let go of their fear of death. "Touch any one of them with the gentle hands of forgiveness, and watch their chains fall away, along with yours." [ACIM T-19.IV.C.2:5] I know the family is accepting this situation as they are calm, gentle, and happy. They are starting to see with the eyes of love. "See him (the patient) throw aside the black robe he was wearing to his funeral, and hear him laugh at death." [ACIM T-19.IV.C.2:6]

Now, the time has come and the patient lets the body go. But he or she has not totally left yet. I see a beautiful white aura floating a few inches above the body as the dying person waits for anyone present to say goodbye and give a final blessing of gratitude and love. Everyone is given salvation by forgiving their loved one of any mistakes that they made and letting Love whisper into their ears, "You too are forgiven."

I ask the family to say goodbye and give a final blessing to their loved one. It is also my final act as a doctor to ask Christ to free this person of this life and take them Home to God. As the spirit of the patient begins to leave, it expands to fill the room and touches all of us with love and peace. Then it is gone because we have just assisted in giving birth of a loved one into heaven.

During this process of dying, "...Love itself has called. And each has been surmounted by the power of the attraction of what lies beyond." [ACIM T-19.IV.D.4:6-7] Everyone is able to see beyond the veil of death into the deep peace of God. Thus, their fears disappear and a loved one is lifted up by all of us to God, who reaches down from heaven and takes the loved one home. Now we have all been blessed by love. Amen.

CHAPTER 7

Meeting God

Wandering

I have wandered this world for a million years. I see only shades of gray darkness all around me. I am alone, not sure where I am going but feeling that I must be somewhere, so I keep walking. I am tired with the burdens of the past upon my back and fearful of the future. I am lost walking on this path, unsure if I am making the right turns or not. Oh how I want to rest, but I cannot. I am restless, so I must keep walking, I must keep searching.

As I travel, I am met by a man in a white robe. His head is shrouded so I cannot see his face. He bids me to stop and rest for a while, lifting the burdens off my back so I can sit more easily. As he removes them, a deep sense of peace descends upon me; it is such a relief to be free of these burdens. He asks where I am going, and reply that I do not know. When I feel rested and ready to walk again, he asks if he can walk with me for a while. I consent, for I am glad to have a travelling companion.

As we start to walk along, he tells me not to pick up my baggage again, as it will only slow us down. Trusting him, I smile in gratitude. Soon I find my pace is slowing and my stride becoming easier, I appreciate new beauty in the colors and shapes of the natural environment; I have never seen such splendor before. Relaxing, I am no longer in any hurry to get anywhere. Finally I stop entirely, in great contentment. I turn to the hooded man and ask, "Who are you?"

"You have been searching for me for a long time," he replies, "and even though you did not know it, I walked next to you. You did not see me because you were blinded to my light. But now you are now ready to see me." He removes his shroud and I am momentarily blinded by the brilliance of his light, the light of Love and Joy. Then I realize I am seeing God with this new vision. His radiance washes me clean.

"You have been travelling on this road of darkness and fear together for a long time," God says. "I have been gently guiding you the entire time, keeping you safe until you were ready to trust me and put your burdens down. You made no wrong turns or mistakes, and you were never lost or alone even though you thought so. But now you can see yourself as you truly are: my Holy Child created by me as a Spirit of light and love. You are free at last to see past the fear that darkens these roads."

As I bask in His light, warmth and love, I realize the clarity of perfect vision. God holds out his hands and takes mine, saying "Your journey is now over and you need not travel again to find me, for here we are one. Your days of walking in the darkness, in doubt and fear, are finished. You will never believe that you are lost again because now you can see me with my light and your perfect vision. You are now home, my innocent child. We will forever walk together in perfect holiness."

Experiencing the Atonement

Now I would like to share with you the second part of the Atonement phase. I entered this spiritual dimension after Christ pulled me through the edge of my separated mind and into the infinity of heaven. Once through, Christ eventually led me to remember the Atonement, i.e., I Am at One with God.

So here is the start of my remembering who I Am, once I was stripped clean of all of my dreams and illusions of Dr. Rod. I first described it in a letter to my friend Dr. Jon Mundy:

Dear Jon,

My mind has just been blasted with the most dazzling white light tonight. I was having dinner at a Chinese restaurant and reading a fortune cookie that said, "Get your mind set, confidence will lead you on." Since that first moment of brightness, the light is still flowing in and through me. My body is vibrating so fast I can barely handle it. I have never seen this in an awakened state but only in deep meditation. Everything I see is glowing with light. My mind is expansive and everything is beautiful to see. Everything looks different now. I was left with this thought:

Forever in love, forever in peace are we are guided by Christ to our true home within. Come, everyone, and join with us, for together we will all find our way home.

Rod

This was the first of many of what I call "light insertions." It is an intense white light that is like a bolt of lightning going through the top of my head, through my body, and into the earth. There is an electrical quality that reminds me of the shock from touching a live wire. This is what I felt a few days later when Christ pulled me into the vastness of infinite space or heaven.

When Christ pulled me into this area of infinity, infinite mind, or Heaven, I was stripped clean of all of my humanistic qualities and became only a pure thought of consciousness, a clear awareness. I felt like corn being shucked. Time and space ended as well, and I was liberated from this dream world of illusion. In this spiritual realm, I returned to my divine essence as a being of light and love, limitless and free of all the constraints of the ego's humanistic world.

In this state, all around me is the vastness of space. It is like standing inside a sphere of infinite dimensions, and the inside of this sphere is lined in a radiant gold-white light. I feel perfectly safe and at home. I also feel the depth of peace beyond comprehension, very powerful, quiet, and still.

"Beyond the body, beyond the sun and stars, past everything you see and yet somehow familiar, is an arc of golden light that stretches as you look into a great and shining circle. And all the circle fills with light before your eyes. The edges of the circle disappear, and what it is in it is no longer contained at all. The light expands and covers everything, extending to the infinity forever shining and with no break or limit anywhere. Within it is everything joined in perfect continuity. Nor is it possible to imagine that anything could be outside, for there is nowhere that this light is not." [ACIM T-21.I.8:1-6]

Christ always stays with me here in this infinite space; we are both pure beings of light held together by a bridge of clear light. Neither Christ nor I has any kind of form; we are awareness only. I know his thoughts and He knows mine. He wants me to become comfortable in our home. Sometimes it feels as if we travel in this space just as two friends do, not talking but walking along the ocean's edge and enjoying each other's company. Sometimes I feel as if a gentle cool breeze is blowing against me as Christ and I walk along inside the sphere of light.

I love being light

I love being light. I have laid my body down for a while and I let it go, to rest in a deep slumber. But my mind has become free again, to return to my true home of infinite brilliance. There is deep solitude, yet a fullness of being. I am one with God. There is the peace and serenity of being within his heart, knowing that I am loved by Him throughout eternity, forever as his loving child.

I love being light. I can see beyond imagination and thought. I see all aspects of the Sonship, forever whole and pure. I let this light flow through me into the world of time and space and bless all that I see. Peace reigns here for a while and all is quiet. All beings are healed in this loving light. We are all whole again in our Father's heart, and as we are held so gently by him, he whispers to us, "I love you."

I love being light. In this purity of mind, whole and healed of any dark thoughts, I remember my True Self as I Am. And as I remember myself, I remember all of you. I see you as you truly are, a thought of love created by our loving Father. You too are light, whole and pure. I see your innocence, your love and your grace. You are brilliant in your love. See yourself as I see you, as God sees you and remember this is who you are, an extension of His Divine Consciousness.

I love being light. My gift to you is this light, so that you too can see and remember who you truly are. Come into this light and you will see that this is so. Wake up! You are a thought of peace, love and joy; a being of light. You are God's holy child.

Integration

Christ continued to guide me in both my spiritual realm and within this everyday dream world. But He now asked me to be more intentional and disciplined in my practice of meditating, studying and watching my thoughts. I had to be more diligent in my "mind training." As my mind opened up, everything became more fluid between the spiritual realm and this humanistic dream world realm.

"This is our first attempt to introduce structure. Do not misconstrue it as an effort to exert force or pressure. You want salvation. You want happiness. You want peace. You do not have them now because your mind is totally undisciplined, and you cannot distinguish joy and sorrow, pleasure and pain, love and fear. You are now learning how to tell them apart. And great indeed will be your reward." [ACIM-W-20.2:1-8]

In addition to more diligence with my practice, Christ wanted me to expand my mind even farther; he wanted me to learn to think with God. I trusted Him so much that this was an easy thing to do. He started to lead me on the most wonderful journey.

With the help of Christ I was joining with the "Thinking of the Universe," aligning my mind with the mind of God. I started to surrender to love and to join my mind with Him. I learned to surrender my will, and I wanted to know only the will of God. In the morning when I woke up or during my meditations, I made a point of surrendering to the divine, asking to know only His will, and then allowing him to connect with me without any demands or restrictions on my part.

I started to edit my thoughts by watching them carefully. This takes practice, but it becomes easier as you let go of controlling the outcome of everything that happens, or the behavior of everyone around you. I learned to become an observer of the world and not be attached to its myriad appearances. Christ would say, "Let me handle it." As I did, calmness and peace would rise within and then flow through me to others. I was becoming the "light of the world," extending love that helped others to see more clearly when I was with them. In essence, the brighter I became, the more light was reflected back to me. As a result of Christ's light, healing would reach all of us as darkness was shined away.

My faith and trust grew as a result of this practice because somehow, every time, everything worked out fine. It was becoming easier to maintain peace within my mind. I started to see the past baggage that I carried with me from this life, as well as the baggage that I carried from my parents' lives and their ancestry. I suppose this is also called Karma. By practicing forgiveness, it is easy to start to let it all go. In addition, when something occurred that upset me, I practiced diligently to remain calm and listen for the voice of Christ.

Painful Distractions

Dear Jon,

There is deep emotional stuff down there deep within my mind that acts like lava under the earth's surface. It bubbles up here and there, causing horrible eruptions of destructive pain.

During a recent kidney stone attack, in my moment of severest pain, I saw my mom's fear as a child. The basis of her fear went far back, beyond the personal history of her own life. I saw death up close and personal, and I was terrified by this sight. But on a second stone attack, I did not lose my sight of Christ's light. The pain was every bit as real but I knew I was okay. I kept my mind on Christ and he helped me with my perception of pain. I have more freedom in my mind as a result.

Eventually I needed surgery to remove the stone. I was very peaceful before surgery and after the operation. Now I am just calm with a touch of happiness in me. My painful blockage has literally been removed. My life energy is flowing again and I am healing.... I know the ego wanted me to react to these two events with the victim mentality and thereby create another block to love. The ego wanted me to reinforce the baggage of pain and suffering, but Christ helped me to forgive and let it go. Already I am forgetting about all of it. I'm staying in the present moment, for here is where I find the most light, peace and healing.

Sincerely,
Rod

As a result of moving through this kidney stone attack, I learned to see through the illusion of this form of temptation, which we call pain here in this dream world, and to maintain my awareness of Christ's presence.

"Pain is a wrong perspective. When it is experienced in any form, it is proof of self-deception. It is not a fact at all. There is no form it takes which will not disappear if seen aright." [ACIM W-190.1:1-4]

Following this painful event, I started to become aware of Christ within all things that I see here in this dream world as well. In my daily life, during these mystical moments, the world transformed and I would see everything as white light.

The World Transformed

I was relaxing one evening and sipping on a glass of wine. As I looked outside into my yard and watched the birds eating the seeds that I had left for them, I suddenly went into the vastness of white light. I was seeing the beauty of infinity there in my mind, at the same time seeing the life in this world. The white light of love was flowing through me and all of them at the same time. I dared not close my eyes because I thought I might lose this sight. It is an amazing dance of light to watch. Everything is white on white infinity — vast, powerful, and loving all at the same time. I felt a deep connection to this infinity and was filled with the joy of knowing who I really am. I felt like I was home where I belong.

In my meditations over the next year I no longer had to do galaxy walks or cross through the curtain of the ego mind. After a few minutes of quieting myself, I would always meet Christ in the vastness of infinite space, and I would just rest in His presence. He was always in front of me. He never had an appearance of any kind, nor did I. I had no thoughts, conversations, or requests of Him, merely enjoying the quietness of peace between us. My meditations were becoming longer and it was very easy to keep my mind centered on His peace; it just takes practice, desire and diligence. What makes it easy is that Christ is right there to help. I learned to surrender, trust, and allow Him freedom in helping me. Christ never really talked with me, until the following event happened during one meditation.

A Red Orb

In this meditation, Christ led me to a very large red orb in the center of clear space. It was a brilliant, huge, scintillating bright red ball that looked alive. He said, "Go ahead and touch it, you are ready." As I studied this large red orb, I hesitated and thought, *This is not a good idea.* But since I was with Christ and I trusted him, I thought it was probably safe to touch it. So I imagined my hand reaching out, and I touched this large red orb. It was then that I heard a very loud crack of thunder and I was hurled back into my chair with incredible force. I immediately woke up and was stunned. What had happened?

I felt completely disconnected from my body and from the world. Nothing made any sense and I was paralyzed. I stayed this way for about twenty minutes before I was able to move my arms and legs again. I felt as if I had a concussion. But as the day wore on, I reconnected with this world.

After this experience, I was able to see my body within the illusion of this world. What I saw was beautiful to behold. My aura was pure white and radiated about one foot from the edge of my body. My heart's aura, usually green, had changed to a brilliant red, the same color as the orb. In fact, it seemed as if the orb was implanted into my heart area. I cannot describe the fullness of the colors but I could actually feel them, and the feeling was that of tremendous love and joy. I have never had this experience again.

Disconnection

Twice I have wanted to leave this world and stay in that

realm of clear space surrounded by white light. The first time I was in Charles Fillmore's Chapel at Unity Village in Missouri, meditating for over an hour. I was in the sphere of light and became overwhelmed with bliss. As a result, I desperately wanted to leave this world behind me. As I seriously contemplated leaving, I felt Christ put his hand on my left shoulder and whisper in my left ear, "Your boys still need you." So I returned to this earthly plane and continued with my daily life of being a dad and a doctor. That was the only time in my life that I heard Christ's voice in my left ear and felt his presence on my left side.

A few years later, I was at home on a Sunday morning meditating and again felt an overwhelming freedom of bliss. I desperately wanted to stay and leave my body behind. I saw a very fine silvery rope about a quarter of an inch thick extending from my mind back to my body. I imagined having spiritual arms and wrapped the rope around my left arm. I knew that if I could just break this rope, I would be free from this world. So I pulled as hard as I could against this rope with both arms, but I could not break it. I tried three times, until it actually felt painful. So I stopped, but I knew that at the right time, this rope would be cut and I would be free.

So I let the rope go and continued to meditate for a while longer. I became satisfied that at least for short while, on a daily basis, I can visit this white sphere of light and be at peace.

Meeting God

As I continued on after that in my daily meditations over the next several years, Christ was always present with me. During one particularly long meditation, Christ asked me, "Do you want to meet God?"

I was stunned by the request and I stopped to think about my answer. I was told so many bad things about God growing up with the Christian faith that I was afraid of his wrath and judgment upon me. But then I thought, how silly of me to have these thoughts, because Christ himself was inviting me to meet our Father. I knew I would be perfectly safe.

In my stillness, I surrendered to God and let go of all my concepts of Him. I let go of all my requests and questions, surrendering my defenses and the armor of old thoughts. I surrendered my will. My only desire was that I truly wanted to meet God. My fear was gone and I stood there naked and with totally open arms.

Once my thoughts began clearing, I waited for God to reveal himself. As I waited, God gently reached out to me. I saw two misty white arms starting to embrace me. God Himself took the final step in this mystical journey of awakening. There was no judgment of me from God and there was no fear on my part. There was a warm feeling of being welcomed home. I could feel a fast electrical vibration occurring in my body and it was a pleasant sensation. My mind had become almost completely quiet.

As God pulled me into Himself, I dissolved into Love's presence; we became One. All thinking stopped and there was only absolute stillness. My mind was now totally wide open, dimensionless, expanded to infinity. When this happened, I experienced several different feelings all at once.

I was first aware of God's tender unconditional love for me, something I cannot fully describe. I have never felt anything like this before. His love flowed freely between us in that instant. Next I sensed the serenity of a deep unshakable peace, "passing all understanding." I also felt His tremendous steadfast power. Finally I perceived a powerful silence that too was beyond description.

But the love that I had awakened to was the most profound feeling of all. Awe, rapture, and ecstasy are words that barely touch the feelings that I was experiencing. These are the feelings and sensations that I felt when I joined with God's unlimited infinite presence.

After this particular meditation, I still felt overwhelmed by these beautiful feelings and I was guided to write the following missive.

I am Caressed by Love

As I relax into a deep meditation, my mind is quiet and my spirit is free. As I begin to float, I feel a gentle touch all around me. My spirit is lifted by God into his loving arms and I am held ever so gently. My body and this world have now faded into the nothingness from which they came. I am surrounded by the white light of peace and I feel God's love for me. I feel safe and secure within his arms. I smile as I look upon God and offer Him my love in return.

As He holds me, He gently strokes my face with the lightness of a feather and whispers in my ears with the sigh of a baby's voice. I am soothed as He gently rocks me. He whispers, "My child, know how much I love you. Know how much I love holding you in my arms. Such delight and pleasure are mine when I can touch you. I am complete and content. You bring me peace, and I quietly cry with the tears of joy because of the love that I feel for you.

"You are born of my love and therefore forever sinless and

perfect in every way. You are holy, pure and innocent. You are my loving child and I am your loving Father. Together, we are eternally inseparable in our perfect love.

"Feel my love for you now as I gently hold you in my arms. Feel the warmth in my heart for you. Feel the pleasure that you give me. Hear the gratitude in my voice as I say to you, thank you my Holy Child. Thank you for giving me your love in return."

As I lay in God's arms, I am cradled in his love. I look into the eyes of love and am comforted. As God's tear touches my cheek, in that moment, I am returned to my innocence and I remember who I truly am.

We are both now melded as one in eternal love, both whole and complete.

As I return to this world, I remember the feeling of being held in God's arms, the warmth of His love and security that I was safe. I am content in knowing that I am forever loved by God Himself. I have surrendered to His Grace, His Love and His Peace. I know and trust that I will be taken care of by my Father. Now, all of these feelings are flowing in my being and my life. I have returned to the oneness of my love with God. In thankful gratitude, I look up and smile. I am at peace.

Embryo of Truth

Following this melding together of my mind with God's, my heart area changed again. Instead of the red aura, I saw a tiny embryo there, surrounded by a white aura.

Later, Christ told me that "This is the Embryo of Truth planted there in your heart by God when you fell asleep and dreamed of being separated from Him. Nurture this Child of

Innocence, and help it to grow by keeping your human mind free of thoughts of judgment, grievance, and fear. Do not build blocks to Love's presence. I will help you. Think as God thinks: I am love, I am truth, I am life, and I am a spiritual being, pure, holy and eternal."

In time, my heart's aura matured into a lotus flower with silvery white petals, and the flower became a beautiful red rose. To this day, years later, this is still what I see within my heart.

Since my first encounter with God, every time I meditate, I now cross easily into the heart of God. We are lovers enjoying each others' companionship. When I am absorbed into God, my awareness is His awareness. I fully enjoy complete communion and Oneness with Him. I experience God's unconditional peace and absolute love as well because I am fully awake now. I remember who I Am, His Son.

I have also learned that God enjoys laughter, joy and dancing. I know the gentle feeling of movement through this great sphere of light with God, feeling as if we are dancing across the heavens. In our wake, we leave behind a colored trail of Stardust.

Dance

How I love to dance with you, my Holy Child. You whom I created from the depth of my being are forever a part of me, and forever loved by me. You are my life, my joy and my happiness.

In timeless eternity, we dance together to the symphonic song that we sing as one. Let the heavens be filled with our music. Let the heavens see our dance as lights, dappled glittering lights, palisading across the sky, our beautiful brush strokes of blended love.

In this dance we are forever secure in our happiness and joy. We are both eternally filled with peace. We are both complete when we are entwined in this embrace, this graceful dance of love.

Changes in my daily life

After these mystical experiences, my daily life changed dramatically. One morning I awoke in peace, and for the first time the world look different. I knew God and saw Him in everything. I have relaxed so much that I no longer feel connected to this world. I know longer aspire for anything in this world, but rather I am now inspired by breathing in God into my heart. I am no longer concerned about this world for I feel loved by God at my deepest level. I live by Grace and I know I'll be taken care of. For I see myself as Christ consciousness or God consciousness, and this consciousness is seeking or attracting to itself all other things in the universe that I need to function. I only need to let go and trust.

Trust Christ

I trust Christ to be there, even when I cannot hear or see Him. I trust Him to do the right thing even though I do not understand the events that I am dealing with. I have limited perception and I have to be careful not to judge the event. If I do, I make the event real and then get trapped by the ego's illusions with all the other people. I do not have all the information to make a correct judgment, so I am likely to make a wrong judgment on my own. My job is simply to treat myself and others with compassion and love. I allow events to unfold but also allow love to flow through me to the world. I forgive myself, you, and the world because I do not want to create a block to love's presence. People need to see the Christ in us so they do not get lost. There are a lot of things I do not understand and that is okay. I just love.*

God in my daily life

Now my daily life is continuously mystical. Things are neither good nor bad, they just are, and I can look through the forms of their illusion to the Oneness of God behind them. As I will explain later, I see two worlds, one with Christ's Vision and one with my limited human vision. I have become an observer of the dramas of the everyday world, and rarely have to react. Whenever an upset is coming my way, I allow it to flow off me, or I step aside. I stay centered in peace and love. Peace has become more important to me than anything else, and all I truly desire is to stay awake and remember who I am.

I now see God all around me and everything looks clean. Peace has come, not with thunder and bright lights, but with a gentle touch on my shoulder and a whisper in my ear. "You are loved!" Such a wonder, such a blessing to know in my heart that I am loved by God and that I am innocent from any thoughts of sin or guilt about offending Him.

"To feel the love of God within you is to see the world anew, shining in innocence, alive with hope, and blessed with perfect charity and love." [ACIM W-189:1.7]

The Gentleness of Love

As I crossed into the deep solitude of my mind, I felt the gentle breeze of grace flowing across me. As I let this pass through me, all thoughts of my body, my life and the world were washed away and I was made clean, returned to my True Self as a pure thought of love. I stood there as a radiant spirit of light, free again of my dream of separation. I was released.

Then in that moment, God reached out and embraced me. Our minds melded into one and I was filled with joy. I was embraced by the gentleness of Love. I was again whole and complete, deeply satisfied with these feelings of profound love and peace for me.

No words were spoken, only the feelings of enjoyment, of total love for me and my total love for God were expressed. There was no distinction between us. Only the Unity of Oneness. I am free and I am complete in God's embrace. All I see is the white light of infinity and of Love. All I feel is deep peace.

To be connected to God on this deep level can only be expressed as awe. Love extended Itself and created a Sonship of Love. And now that I remember who I am, I realize that I am part of that Love, loving Itself. This flow of love is so gentle and sweet, so healing and kind, and welcomes me back to Itself without judgment. I am home now with my Father, safe in His Love. How long we floated in this love I cannot say, for time has no meaning in Eternity.

But part of me is still tied to this world, and so I come back. And each time I do, Love comes with me to bless and heal all that I see.

Now I am thinking of you, my friends, and I want to share with you this truth. There is a light in you that I see, there in your heart. It is a pure white light of love, connected to the Divine. You are in truth as pure and holy as am I, an extension of God Himself. He loves you with unconditional love and He is there in your heart, ready to remind you of His love for you. Be still, look in your heart and trust Him to embrace you in His arms again. He will remind you of these truths that you are His holy child, forever pure and innocent, and forever loved by Him.

The ineffable knowledge of God

From these experiences I now "know God." There is no more doubt in my mind that I am an individualized extension of God consciousness, and that we are one. This "noetic" characteristic is an aspect of being a mystic. God has become my constant companion now, and whether I call him Christ, the Holy Spirit, or God, these words are all synonymous. In the word know is now, and it is in the Now that I find God. There is no past or future in knowing God.

Another mystical characteristic I became aware of was the feeling of oneness with everyone and everything around me. Dr. Carl Jung described this as characteristic as "oceanic." Simply stated, we are all connected by God's love.

One day, I was walking to the grocery store and I had a moment of clarity, a "Holy Instant." I dissociated from my body and watched it walk into the store. What was amazing is that I could walk and do all the things I needed to do, but remain disconnected. I could see all the love flowing through me to everything and everyone around me. I felt such peace and contentment within my mind. People around me stopped and smiled. I could tell they felt the love radiating from me so they became very peaceful as well. I could see their spirit resonate and light up in return to the love that they were feeling. I smiled back. It is such a wonderful feeling to connect to everyone this way. We are in total communion as one with the love of God flowing through all of us.

Uncovering Your Light

You can do all these things that I have done, for you too are a mystic in your heart. You too are the "Light of the World." You have merely covered your light with a body suit, a personality, and a life. You were taught by the ego to misidentify with this worldly reality and to believe that God is separate from you. But you can unlearn that false identity with desire, the help of Christ, and practice. Say "Yes," when God calls and you will find his love within your heart. In the meantime, here are God's words to you:

Holy Child of Mine

Holy Child of mine, feel my love for you, there in your heart. Feel my loving touch and know how much I love you. You are my Holy Child, forever pure in your heart, innocent as a newborn child, pure as freshly fallen snow. How I love you, my Holy Child. I am filled with love and joy for you. Forever pure in this love, you are a being of light. Look into your mind and see that this is so. This is my will for you.

Let my peace descend upon you. Then let my love shine away the darkness of separation in your mind and you will be sanctified. For this, I extend my love and gratitude to you because now I too am whole and complete again.

So remember my love and let my Grace flow into your life. You are my Holy Child.

Inseparable forever in this love we stand. I will bless you and keep you safe. You are a part of me and I of you. In joy and peace, rest in my love.

All is well.

CHAPTER 8

Extending Love

*A*s I relaxed into the quiet infinity of Heaven, my thoughts of this world faded from my mind and I was free again to be with God. He comes as easily to me now as two friends who meet on the street. He cradles me with His gentle embrace and we become One in love. How sweet and pleasurable is the feeling of love flowing through my mind and my heart. How pure is His love for me. How deep is the peace that he gives me. All I see is beauty, love and kindness. Pure silence is all I hear. I am content to rest here and enjoy being loved by God. For a while, my dreaming is gone and I know I am home safe, warm and at peace. There are no thoughts in my mind as I look at the infinity of Heaven with God. I have lost myself in His love. I am as He is, pure infinite love.

We rest together for a while, how long I cannot say for eternity has no time, only freedom. I bask in this union with God and enjoy the feelings of peace and love.

As I see each of you in my mind, love flows between us and we too become One. In your heart, I see the white light of love glowing brightly and I see you as you truly are; the child of love, the child of peace, the child of light. You are the Christ Child. Pure, clean and innocent, the offspring of a very loving parent.

We are all united together in love with God. Born from His love, we celebrate our birth. His Love has entered your life and He has given you several gifts. These are the gifts of love, peace and joy. Know that forever you are His holy child and that you are eternally loved, never to be alone from Him.

After perhaps a year of these meditations and experiences, I entered the third phase of my mysticism, "the extension of Love." One day God spoke to me and asked me very clearly, "Will you help me in healing the Sonship?" He wanted my help in extending His love back to those who were still dreaming of being separated from him. Please remember, though, that I am no guru, no prophet nor saint. I am, in fact, nobody.

God has no way to communicate with us, so he uses intermediaries like me as a channel or a translator for Him. There are thousands of intermediaries who have been helping in this process for thousands of years. When God speaks to me, it is the Holy Spirit's voice that I hear inside my head. I relay the message to whomever I'm speaking with. People hear my human voice and think that it is me who is speaking to them, but this is not so. Other times, I write down what I hear such as the short poems presented in this text.

Therefore, I believe it is the function of God within me to help heal the world, bless mankind, and help those with illnesses, death and lack in their lives. Thus I am merely a translator or conduit for the extension of Love's presence in this world, on God's behalf and yours.

I will describe three different experiences where His love extended through me. First, He asks me to help "Bless the World." For the second type of healing, God asks me to help those who are stuck in what I call the "Etheric Realm." The third type of healing occurs here in this world where people ask me for help with a problem within their lives here.

The first two healing meditations that I practice always start when I have merged with God for a while. We are joined in silent communication just enjoying each other's company. I am always blessed first. In these meditations I experience profound love, joy and peace. Then I usually feel but sometimes hear God's request for help in healing the world. God always asks me first if I will help Him, and I always say "Yes!" He has never taken me for granted nor barged into my thoughts. He is very respectful of me. As I open my heart, His Grace flows through it and covers the world in love.

For my third type of healing, I am awake and interacting with someone here in this world. I calm my mind and become extremely quiet so I can connect with God. Once connected, I allow God to communicate through me. As I discuss someone's concerns with them, the presence of his love is still expressed from my heart to whom I am talking with as well as to those around me. Therefore we are communicating on two levels, one with our human senses and one with our spiritual senses. Everyone resonates with this and knows that what I'm saying is the truth because the words are from the Holy Spirit and not from me. These individuals as well as those around us become calm and feel peaceful as a result. Now they are open to God's healing Grace.

Blessing the world

This is my most common healing meditation for the world. During my participation in blessing the world with God, my mind expands to infinity. With my pure spiritual vision, I see the earth as a large gray ball and in the distant background, space appears as a soft, off-white blanket. I do not see stars or other planets nor any other colors. I have never seen the earth as the astronauts do with their human vision from outer space.

I start to see a clear outline of my body and within the area of my heart, there is a wide open channel. Moving through this channel I see a milky-white, sweet, thick and creamy light flowing into all the cracks and crevices of this world. I can also sense this movement and it is delicious to me. I cannot drink enough of this liquid love, it was so sweet and satisfying. I feel very honored and humbled to be a bearer of this "White Light of Love," this liquid love that I also call "Grace." I never once told God where to send His light. That would be like telling water where to flow. I just observe the flow of this liquid love to where it is needed. I make it a point, however, to keep my mind as clean and as pure as I can. I do not want to contaminate this beautiful white light. I have learned to step aside with my thoughts and just let His love flow through me.

As God's Grace flows, His Love and Joy fill the earth and then healing takes place within it. The earth changes from a light gray shade to a brilliant pure white. In this state of mind, all I can hear is silence and I see only radiant white light. I am truly the "Light of the World" because all I see is His white light flowing through me. This cleansing process eventually will lead all of us to Truth. It is the flow of God's Grace that washes our world clean and helps us to wake up from this dream state. And I know that God's endless love will last forever. This dream state and this world will end. It's only a matter of time.

In a different, more personal meditation, I see my astral

body against the infinity of heaven. I start to repeat "I am the light of the world" while holding the earth and all people in the light of love. In this way I bless the world for a while as the white light of peace encircles it. I start to see many people travelling and they all stop for a moment to bask with me in this light. As they do, I see each person's aura change from a faint light gray hue to the clearness of a flawless diamond. The world was free of insanity for a few seconds while as everyone paused to receive God's Love. During these times, I know that not a single death occurred on this planet.

Sometimes during these meditations, when I look at my astral body, there is an intense white light that starts at the base of my spine and it explodes about a foot above my head like fireworks. Then everyone is showered in this brilliant white light. Instead of being clear, they all become a vivid white entity as well. This is followed by a very powerful feeling of oneness and love for all. This is like a spiritual orgasm. It is very intense and beautiful!

These are my two most common meditations that I experience. From them, I remember that we are all clear light beings, thoughts of love, and extensions of God himself. We are individualized Christ consciousness and all we have to do is wake up. We are not these false, dark illusions that we identify with in this dream world.

I am glad that I can help others stop their imagining and wake up. I am glad that for a moment, they remember that they are still one with God. There is such tremendous joy for all when this occurs.

Our World Made Clean

One week I was troubled with feelings of deep anger and fear. I did not know why until I asked Christ why, and He responded: "Our world has been covered over in these feelings and it is crying for help. It is bleeding with pain and suffering. These were not your feelings but those of the world." Hearing this, I decided to help Christ heal the world.

So I went into deep meditation with the intention of healing the world. I saw our world as it is now: a sooty, dirty, gray globe. In the background was the white light of our spiritual realm.

I went into my heart and opened it up to God's Love. As I felt this love starting to flow, I watched this love cover and wash over our world. I started to see the vague faces of people and places where there was extra fear and pain. I saw those we consider murderers and those we consider victims. I saw their pain and washed them all with love. I also saw those left behind grieving for their loss of loved ones. I saw the global fear of people everywhere. I let love wash them all as well. Everyone's heart was touched with God's compassion and love. Everyone's innocence started to shine within them again and they began to feel peace. Their darkness of fear and pain was being washed away by love.

I saw the rips and tears in the fabric of this world and placed a few stitches here and there. Open wounds and barriers that seemed impossible to cross were closed. Love could now flow freely around the world.

As I continued to let love flow, the world started to change. The black ink of fear dripped off and vanished into nothingness. The world suddenly turned pure white and radiated love. It was beautiful to see; peace had come again. The world was washed clean with God's love and fear was replaced by love. For a while, peace reigned.

Help me now as we continue the healing process for our world. When thoughts of anger or fear or hatred enter your mind, do not react to them, but instead let them flow through you. For under these emotions is a cry for love. Let God's love flow through you into your mind, your life and into this world and to those who need it so much. You are the light of the world. Be a miracle worker today and let your light shine. Help God shine away the darkness. Together, we will light up the world and bring it peace.

Blessing the Sonship

Following my blessing of the earth with God, my second meditation changes from time to time. I am in a different realm, a giant sphere of infinite dimensions. In the center of this sphere there is clear space, and the background is like twilight in a starless sky. I call this the "Etheric Realm."

Sometimes, I see a single long line of clear individuals that extend backwards as far as I can see. These people are on my left side, and I assume this to be the past. When I look towards my right side I can see all the individuals who have yet to be born. This line represents the future and it too extends into infinity. Altogether I call this the "Timeline of Life." I am in the middle of this timeline and if I look down, I see all the individuals who have journeyed with me in my present lifetime. There is a teardrop shape within this Timeline that represents my life. We are all connected by a single strand of life. God's love flows from my heart through this strand to all those who are in the past and future. Everyone changes from a clear aura to a light white aura; it happens in an instant. I know that they have been blessed, touched and changed by God's love for them.

Other times I see millions of people standing on an infinite plane in this etheric realm. Their auras are clear and they're all looking towards me. I see the outline of Christ in the shape of a human being. He has a white aura and is always on my right side. We are standing on a slight elevation above all of these people. I am standing on top of the hills with my arms held down and opened outwards. I am bowing my head.

In this spiritual dimension, I am again aware of my oneness with God. I allow God to extend His light through me as everyone looks to see this white light of love flowing from my heart. All of the people around me are washed clean in this light.

We are all caressed by love and held ever so gently by God's touch. I am so humbled and honored to be able to do this work and give this gift of love. We are all so intensely blessed and so deeply loved by God and once we remember this, our world becomes insignificant.

A few individuals have accepted God's love in this instant, and in so doing they have lightened up, letting go of their baggage from previous lives. They leave and return home to heaven above. Individuals who leave are like fireflies; they are bright for a moment and then they are gone. All follow the same path of ascending up and towards the right, being guided home by God.

I know that even those who choose to stay behind are still loved by God. I see their clear auras in the shape of people, yet they are not moving. They just seem to be silently standing in place waiting for something to happen. For whatever reason, they are finding it difficult to let go and accept God's love for them.

But Christ is still with them, allowing them time to rest, wake up and remember who they are. This is a very gentle, slow, loving process. I know they will be healed and taken care of because of Christ's presence. They are never alone nor forsaken.

I know that eventually in time all will wake up and become free, because Christ is still there with them even as I leave.

"... For the Lord your God goes with you; he will never leave you nor forsake you." [Deut. 31:6, NIV]

Bending the Dream

A young lady came in the emergency room with a migraine headache of three days duration. She was severely dehydrated from nausea and vomiting, and in a great deal of pain. When I examined her, we immediately went into a dimensionless reality. I saw her aura; she was holding a dark black orb in her right hand and extending it towards me. Her message was: "See, this is what I am, I am this pain and suffering."

As I looked at her holding this black orb out to me, I silently replied, "You are wrong, for you are the Light of Christ. I see you as whole and complete, free of pain and suffering. What you believe you are is merely a terrible dream of suffering and pain."

I added, "Let me help you bend your dream and you will see that this is so." I then relaxed and opened my heart. I let the love of Christ flow between us and in that instant, she was healed.

She then sat up on the gurney and smiled at me. She said,

"It's gone. It's really gone!" She gave me a hug and then left the ER.

Blessing individuals

Over the years since I started practice in 1989, several people asked me to pray for specific healings. At first, I would use affirmations and ask God to heal someone's particular problem. This usually failed. Eventually I realized what I was doing wrong.

Now I no longer attempt such "magic tricks." When someone asks me for healing, I meditate to become still, making no affirmations or denials. Thoughts about the problem that an individual has may come to mind, but I let them flow through and attach no significance to them. I call instead upon Christ and wait for the "frame shift" to occur. When it does, I know I am connected to a higher form of consciousness.

It is God's presence that connects us and helps us all to remember that we are one in His love — and in that love we are perfect, whole, and healthy. To paraphrase Christ, "I of my own self can do nothing. It is the Father in me who doeth the works." [John 5:30, KJV]

To reiterate, I turn to Christ in true prayer and I reconnect with Him. I empty my mind of requests or thoughts of the individual or their problems. I then extend His love from my heart to those that need help. Now healing occurs for them as their consciousness is raised up, or resurrected into Christ consciousness. By changing their perception of the problem, the blocks to love's presence are removed, and these individuals are reminded of their True Self. Once they realize this, their problems automatically dissolve back into the nothingness from which they came, for God's light is shining in them now. In the physical world, this is seen as a demonstration of healing. But in truth, they became aware of their Christ consciousness and that is all that really matters.

I am merely a bridge for Christ so that He may act through me and help those that ask. I leave the outcome of the problem up to God.

Seeing the problem and solution

A young man was admitted to the hospital with a knee infection, nausea and vomiting. Despite medications including antibiotics, he continued to deteriorate. His mother was becoming frantic and asked the doctors why he wasn't getting better. They helplessly replied, "We don't know."

I was asked to visit them and the minute I walked into the room, Christ walked in with me. Everyone became aware of His presence and started to relax. Also as a result of his guidance, I immediately knew that this young man was on the wrong medications and I knew what his real medical problems were. Christ was so gentle and kind in talking through me to them. He explained to everyone, hospital staff included, which medications to use and what this young man's underlying medical problems were. Christ also told me that He would guide the doctors into using the correct medical treatments for this young man.

At the end of my first visit, I walked over to this young man and told him that he was going to be fine, that he would heal quickly and be going home soon. I could feel love's presence flowing through me to everyone during this time, but also specifically to him. I felt a deep connection with him and I knew he was healed.

Once the doctors changed his medications, he quickly recovered and was sent home two days later. I saw him a month afterwards and he was vibrant with life, totally recovered.

Christ in the Middle East

A group of individuals were going to the Middle East to hold a peace conference. They were going into a hot war zone, and a friend asked me to pray for them.

I went into a quiet meditation and held everyone in the light of God. In my mind, I could see where they were going to pray and sing. I saw Christ as a brilliant white figure standing in the middle of them. I could see the soldiers turn towards Christ, and upon hearing the music, they laid their weapons down. Christ's presence was real to them even at this distance.

Many months later, I talked to the director about his experience and though he did not experience Christ's presence, he felt safe and protected. During this time, they could hear that all of the gunfire had ceased. In the center of their stage, there was a white flagpole and they all touched it while they sang and prayed.

He also said he heard a wolf howling off in the distance. I just smiled to myself, because one of my spirit guides is a large gray wolf who protects me.

Deeper Healing

An elderly woman had entered the active dying phase of her life. Several family members were present, consumed by fear and anger. When I was contacted by the facility, in that instant I heard the voice of Christ say, "Go to them." So, I left one nursing facility and went to the patient's bedside in another facility.

Once there, it was obvious the patient had pneumonia in addition to her other medical problems. As Christ was with me, I stepped aside and let Him speak. His presence is so powerful during these times that it's almost palpable. Everyone turned to me and I could see that anger, doubt and fear was going to be haunting them the rest of their lives about their mother's death, without His help.

But with Christ present, everyone calmed down and started to listen to what He had to say. Christ explained to her family that we would do this last "Hail Mary Pass" with medication, and reassess her the following day. If she didn't turn the corner by tomorrow morning, she would never do so. The family was greatly relieved and peace was now in the room with them. Before I left the facility, I started the patient on several aggressive life-saving medications to help her breathe and treat her pneumonia.

When I examined her the following morning, my medicines had failed and it was clear to me that my patient was going to die. But since Christ had been present all through the night, everyone was calm and peaceful and quietly saying goodbye. As they were letting go, with the families' consent, I stopped all her medications and my patient left later in the afternoon. I knew she was in Christ's hands. The family was not going to be left with memories of doubt, fear and anger. Questions of "what if?" would not haunt them the rest of their lives. They knew that their mother was okay. A deeper healing occurred and the family members were all thankful and at peace.

Extending love to Groups

I have had the experience of extending love to large groups of people. I can be at work, shopping, or in traffic when this happens. I suddenly relax and then notice that any chaos or noise around me quiets down. I feel the presence of Christ radiating from my heart, and His peace reigns.

Once when I was doing my rounds on a dementia unit, I saw all the patients in my mind as trapped in their bodies, unable to let go. They were trapped in a kind of feedback loop that prevented them from communicating. I stood there filled with love and compassion, for we were all connected via our mind. The noisiness of the place settled down for a while as the blanket of peace and love settled on us. I just stood there in awe, appreciating a "holy instant" in which we were all blessed.

At other times when I'm driving or walking around in public, I see the darkness of the ego coming towards me from different directions in many different forms. When I see this, I am able to bring the white light of love with me, to shine away the darkness of the illusions of all these different egos. All deceptions simply fade away and I see everyone's light. People smile at me in gratitude because suddenly they experience God's healing touch of love and feel His peace.

"Your peace surrounds me, Father. Where I go, Your peace goes there with me. It sheds its light on everyone I meet. I bring it to the desolate and the lonely and the afraid. I give Your peace to those who suffer pain, or grief, or loss, or think they are bereft of hope and happiness. Send them to me, my Father. Let me bring Your peace with me. For I would save Your Son, as is Your Will, that I may come to recognize my Self." [ACIM W-245:1-8]

In conclusion

I extend God's love now and I am here only to be truly helpful. I feel such delight to be of service, deeply honored and humbled to be asked by God to help heal the Sonship, no matter which dimension I find them in. I have learned to step aside and let His Grace flow to everyone. I let problems or conditions go, for they are all simply illusions, no matter where they are or what form they take.

As His love flows through me to others, I feel full, content and joyful. I experience the movement of His Grace through me. It is sweet and delicious. I notice a subtle, fast vibration occurring within my body, and it is extremely pleasurable. Through my spiritual vision, I see everyone washed clean; we are all as pure and innocent as a newborn babe. We are indeed the offspring of a loving Father, for this is who we are in the light of Truth.

Compared to my medical career, my new job is quite simple. I help people choose once again to recall that we are all as God created us, an extension of Himself. We remember that we are all forever one with Him in His Love.

"And so again we make the only choice that can be made: we choose between illusions and the truth, or pain and joy, or hell and Heaven. Let our gratitude unto our teacher fill our hearts as we are free to choose our joy instead of pain, our holiness in place of sin, the peace of God instead of conflict, and the light of Heaven over the darkness of the world." [ACIM W-190.11:1-2]

The Flow of God's Grace

How sweet is the feeling of God's liquid love, which I call Grace, flowing through my heart into everyone. With my spiritual vision, I see others immersed in this liquid Love, His perfect love for all. This Grace is freeing everyone from the tombs of their darkness and fear, experienced as lack, pain, limitations, disease and death. They are diverse appearances of guilt and are based on the false thought that we are separated from God.

I am opening the way for our imprisoned splendor to be released. As this liquid Grace flows, it washes everyone clean. Everybody feels this as forgiveness and their blindness is removed. A miracle of healing occurs as God Himself does His mighty works through me.

With a new enlightened perception, everyone sees clearly now that they have no problems, and remembers that God has always been there within our hearts. It was all just a dream of illusions and curtains of darkness.

We are liberated now, and ascend to Heaven to fully experience God's love for us once again. We all remember that "I and my Father are One." In gratitude we say, "Thank you Father for showering us in your liquid love and making us clean, so that we could see you and find our way home again to our salvation."

Everyone knows now that they will live forever in God's eternal love, experience His total joy and always remain in His eternal peace. Amen.

EPILOGUE

Ripples

Peace, love and Joy abide in me. I give these gifts freely to you for you to enjoy. Let no thoughts of self reject them. Welcome them. Savor them, for they will bring miracles to your life and restore you to your Christhood. When you are resurrected, then pass them on. Cast the pebbles of these gifts far and wide into the ocean of your life, and their ripples will be felt for generations to come.

Now I walk between two worlds. I see with my human sight all the things that you see in a world of form, duality, and separation. I see the innocence in good and bad and everything in between. But I am no longer attached to what I see nor do I believe in the reality of it. I have become a transparent observer. I am merely watching a movie that I created in my mind and I wish to see it played out. I created a character, a concept or ego that is composed of a body, a personality and a life. In this dream world, I am called Dr. Rod Chelberg. But now I just sit back and watch the movie I made unfold in this dream world.

I also see with a new spiritual vision a different, beautiful world of light, harmony, peace and Oneness. I see the flow of love to everything, inanimate or alive. I see everything as God. "God is... and then we cease to speak." In this dream world, God manifests as me, you, and everyone else. We are all one extension of God, a thought of love in His holy mind. I am complete within His Divine love, radiating the fullness of these emotions into the world and seeing reflected back to me only what God sees, our holiness. How beautiful we all are when we are washed in the light of God.

A New Path

In this process of awakening and remembering who I Am as Christ consciousness, I had to unlearn the world taught to me by the ego and relearn my True Identity. For this process to occur, I asked Christ for help. And when I did, He became my teacher.

As I became more aware of Christ consciousness within me, I was learning to feel, hear and see God manifesting everywhere I looked. This brought me comfort and peace.

With diligence and practice, peace now comes to me with every step I take. I walk on this new path with God in perfect holiness. I am co-creating my world with Christ as my guide instead of the ego as my guide. I'm all done having crash-and-burn experiences!

"Between these paths there is another road that leads away from loss of every kind, for sacrifice and deprivation both are quickly left behind. This is the way appointed for you now. You walk this path as others walk, nor do you seem to be distinct from them, although you are indeed. Thus can you serve them while you serve yourself, and set their footsteps on the way that God has opened up to you, and them through you." [ACIM W-155. 5:1-4]

Since I asked God many years ago to get to know Him and to find peace, I was gently taught over the next twenty years that what I was seeking for was already there within me. "I Am That I Am" was my true name. And I know that "The peace of God, which passeth all understanding, shall keep your hearts and minds through Christ Jesus" (Philippians 4:7. KJV) was the deep peace that I found within my heart. I no longer needed to search for peace anywhere else. I am done. I am fulfilled and content. I am awake now and I know who I am, an extension of the Divine or Christ consciousness.

I learned that my fears were not real, only false beliefs taught to me by ego. They were meant to block my awareness of Love's presence and maintain my belief that God and I were separate. I now understand that my fears were only illusions and nothing more. When I feel some distress, have questions or doubt in my life, I meditate and ask for Christ's guidance. As I rest in His presence, I am touched by Him and we become one. His gentle touch and calm voice comfort me, and I relax. Then I am flooded with assurances and promises that are backed by Divine Authority. As I allow God's Grace to shine into my life, I am lifted out of these discords and inharmonies and enter into a state of illumination. I have found freedom from my fears and limitations. It is such a nice way to live, by His Grace.

"This is the day of peace. You rest in God, and while the world is torn by winds of hate your rest remains completely undisturbed. Yours is the rest of truth. Appearances cannot intrude on you. You call to all to join you in your rest, and they will hear and come to you because you rest in God. They will not hear another voice than yours because you gave your voice to God, and now you rest in Him and let Him speak through you." [ACIM W.109.4:1-6]

In time, I became comfortable surrendering my ego's will and listening for my "marching orders or God's Will," to be revealed to me for each day. As I said earlier, I trust Him to be there and I know that He will protect me and lead me safely through each day. I still feel Christ's constant presence on my right side where ever I go. If I am not sure of what to do, I stop and re-center myself. I wait until I hear His voice giving me direction.

I also think constantly that I am truth, I am love, and I am peace. In all my activities, I extend His goodwill, expressing His love, peace, and compassion to all that I meet. I try to help light everyone's way so that they too may feel God's presence and enjoy His peace.

Finally, I no longer live in the past or the future. I live in the "Now," as this is the only real moment I have and it is here where God resides. Heaven is not sometime in the future, it is here in this instant. There is nothing for me to do anymore except to listen, relax, and allow His Grace to flow into my life. As a result the pure love of God harmonizes within me, in my life and in my world. Everything is flowing beautifully in this white river of love.

White Rain Falling

As I sit in the glass room of my home, I look out and see the gentle snow falling on the earth this winter day. This white rain is washing everything clean. All is quiet and still. I am content to sit here and enjoy this scene and be at peace. Such beauty is covering our earth and repainting it a golden white, the color of God's love.

Then, within my solitude, God gently knocks and asks

Epilogue

my welcome. I simply nod yes and He settles beside me. No words are spoken. We become one in spirit and simply enjoy each other's company while we watch the white rain falling on this winter day. There is no need to talk, but only to enjoy our deep friendship and love for each other and all that we see.

Time has stopped as we experience the mystery unfolding before us. Everything is becoming pure and clean again as it is washed by this white rain. Everything is returning to its innocence and its essence of pure love. I too am becoming part of this process, as I harmonize with God and the world around me. We are all becoming one in the light of His golden white love.

As I sit here quietly with God, I extend our love to each of you. May you and your life be healed and washed clean again, just like this white rain is cleaning our world. Then, as I do, enjoy the peace of God and see his Grace unfolding in your life. Now be at peace, and know that "All is well."

ACKNOWLEDGMENTS

I never would have written anything had it not been for the help and encouragement of Jon Mundy, PhD. He was always so knd to me, and helped pull me out of a deep resistance to expressing myself in public. I am a medical doctor and a scientist, for God's sake! As a profession, we do not talk about mystical or spiritual events.

I was hesitant to tell people about what I was seeing and hearing. Jon assured me that I was not going crazy because of the love that was growing within my heart and that this love needed to be expressed to those around me. He invited me to speak with him in several public forums, and I considered this to be a tremendous honor as he is a national speaker. He also supported me and my writings by publishing several of my articles and poems in "Miracles Magazine."

I and the world owe so much to you, Jon. Thank you so much my friend!

I also wish to thank Rev. Vicki Thomas. She too gave me a lot of much-needed encouragement, support and friendship. She asked me to speak in her home during several presentations for her group "Open Doors." Vicki,, like Jon, provided a safe venue for me to express myself and open up. She is a lovely, dear friend with a great heart.

A special word of thanks to my spiritual mentor, Joel Goldsmith. I found his teaching to be so helpful. He is so kind and patient. Though he is not here in physical form, he is very much alive in spirit and I enjoy his company.

Finally, a note of gratitude to Dr. Ken Wapnick. Though he too is gone from this physical plane, he is very much alive in spirit and would guide me artfully to many of the quotes that I used in this text. I could literally feel his presence and hear his voice as he did this. He too is a great teacher and has become another close friend.

I consider myself lucky to have so many great friends and teachers in my life. Our world is better because of them.